INTERMITTENT FASTING
FOR WOMEN OVER 50

TURN BACK THE AGING CLOCK, FIGHT MENOPAUSE, SLIM YOUR WAISTLINE WITH 174 HEALTHY AND TASTY RECIPES // TAILORED 30-DAY MEAL PLAN

CATHERINE B.REED

CONTENTS

INTRODUCTION

Fasting is the practice of going without food or water for a prolonged amount of time. It could improve your well-being depending on how it is handled. Fasting is usually undertaken for dietary, political, or religious reasons. Intermittent fasting is a common practice that involves cycling through periods of feeding and fasting. Many diets prioritize what to eat, but intermittent fasting emphasizes when to eat.

Intermittent fasting is when you eat during specific hours of the day. Martin Berkhan popularized this style of intermittent fasting, which is where the name comes from. Fasting for a set number of hours per day, or consuming just one meal a couple of times a week, will aid in weight loss. Scientific research also suggests that there are many health advantages to intermittent fasting. Mark Mattson, Ph.D., a neuroscientist at Johns Hopkins University, has studied intermittent fasting for around 25 years. He claims that our bodies have adapted to going without meals for many hours, days, or even weeks. Before man learned to plant, there were gatherers and hunters who adapted to survive without eating over lengthy periods. They needed to because hunting games, and collecting nuts and berries required a lot of time and commitment. It was also simpler to maintain a healthier weight 50 years earlier. "There were no phones, only T.V. programs shut off at 11 p.m.; people avoided consuming before they went to bed," says Christie Williams, M.S., R.D.N., a dietitian at Johns Hopkins. "The portions were much lower. More citizens exercised and played outdoors, getting more exercise in general. But television, the telephone, and other forms of entertainment are now accessible 24 hours a day, seven days a week. We remain up later to watch our favorite series, play sports, and talk on the phone. We spend the whole day and much of the night sitting and snacking."

Obesity, heart failure, type 2 diabetes, and other diseases may also be worsened from consuming so many calories and doing so little. Intermittent fasting has been seen in scientific trials to change these phenomena further. Give this book a try; you will learn a lot about intermittent fasting and its tremendous benefits that can improve your lifespan and health, even when you are in your 50s.

CHAPTER 1: INTERMITTENT FASTING'S BASICS

Intermittent fasting is a way of eating, not a diet. It is a method of planning your meals so that you get the best out of them. Intermittent fasting does not alter your eating habits; however, it alters the timing of your meals.

If you think about it, intermittent fasting makes a lot of sense. Enzymes in our stomach break down the food we consume and then become molecules in the bloodstream. Sugar and processed grains (white flour and rice) are easily broken down into sugar, which our cells use for fuel. If our bodies do not need it all, it is processed as energy in our fat cells. On the other hand, sugar will only reach our cells by insulin, a hormone produced by the pancreas. Insulin is a hormone that carries sugar into our fat cells and holds it there.

Our insulin levels will decrease during meals if we do not eat, and our fat cells will be able to release their accumulated sugar to be used as energy. If we allow our insulin levels to decrease, we lose weight. The whole point of intermittent fasting is to make insulin levels drop low enough and for long enough that fat is burned off.

Why is it worthwhile to change when you are eating?

Most importantly, it is a smart way to get healthy without being on a fad diet or severely restricting your calorie intake. In reality, when you first start intermittent fasting, you will aim to maintain a steady calorie intake. Most people consume larger meals in a shorter period. Intermittent fasting is often a healthy way to retain muscle mass when gaining weight. The predominant reason people pursue intermittent fasting is to inevitably lose weight. Perhaps notably, since it takes relatively little behavior adjustment, intermittent fasting is one of the best methods for losing unwanted weight while maintaining a healthy one. This is a positive thing, as it implies intermittent fasting falls under the category of "easy enough to perform, but significant enough to make a difference."

1.1 How does intermittent fasting work?

To understand how intermittent fasting contributes to fat loss, we must first understand the distinction between the feeding and fasted states. When the body digests and absorbs food, it is in a fed condition. The fed condition typically occurs when you start eating and lasts three to five hours as the body absorbs and digests the meal you just consumed. Since your insulin levels are elevated while you are in the fed state, it is difficult for your body to burn fat. During that time frame, the body reaches a condition recognized as the post-absorptive state, which is a fancy way of suggesting that it is not processing a meal. The post-absorptive condition continues before you reach the fasted state, which is 8 to 12 hours from your last meal. Since insulin levels are low, it is much simpler for your body to burn fat while you are fasting.

FASTING

Fasting allows the body to burn fat that was previously unavailable during the fed state. Our bodies are rarely in this fat-burning condition, and we do not enter the fasted state until 12 hours after the last meal. This explains why many people who begin intermittent fasting lose weight without altering their diet, amount of food consumed, or exercise frequency. Fasting induces a fat-burning condition in your body that you seldom achieve with a regular eating schedule. Intermittent fasting could be done in various ways, but they all revolve around choosing daily eating and fasting times. For example, you might consider eating for only eight hours a day and fasting for the rest. Alternatively, you might opt to consume just one meal a day, two days a week. There are a variety of intermittent fasting plans to choose from. According to Dr. Mattson, after some time without carbohydrates, the body's sugar reserves are depleted and begin to burn fat. This is alluded to as 'metabolic flipping' by him.

"Most Americans eat in their waking hours, but intermittent fasting is in comparison to their usual eating pattern," Dr. Mattson states. "If somebody eats three meals a day with desserts and does not exercise, they're living on some calories and are not burning their fat reserves any time they eat."

Intermittent fasting functions by extending the time from when the body burns off the calories from your last meal and starts burning fat.

Lower metabolism, achy muscles, decreased body mass, and even sleep problems make it more challenging to lose weight after the age of 50. Simultaneously, losing fat, including harmful belly fat, will significantly lower the risk of major health problems, including heart attacks, diabetes, and cancer. Of course, as you get older, the chances of contracting a variety of diseases rise. When it comes to weight reduction and the risk of developing age-related illnesses, intermittent fasting, especially for women over 50, can be a virtual fountain of youth in certain cases.

A quick overview of intermittent fasting plans:

This eating style can be approached in a variety of ways. Any method can be successful, but determining which one works better for you is a personal decision.

Intermittent fasting is done in a variety of ways; some popular methods include:

- The 16/8 method
- The 5:2 diet
- Eat Stop Eat
- Alternate day fasting
- The Warrior Diet
- Spontaneous meal skipping
- Crescendo fasting

Before beginning intermittent fasting, make sure to consult your doctor. The procedure itself is easy if you have his or her approval. You may use a regular solution, which limits daily eating to one six-to-eight hour span. For example, you might try 16/8 fasting, which involves eating for eight hours and fasting for sixteen. Dr. Williams is a supporter of the everyday routine, claiming that most individuals find it simple to adhere to this pattern over time.

Another method, known as the 5:2 solution, entails eating five times a week. You only eat one 500–600 calorie meal on the remaining two days. For instance, suppose you wanted to eat normally any day of the week, you would only exclude Mondays and Thursdays, which would be your one-meal days.

Fasting over extended amounts of time, such as 24, 36, 48, and 72 hours, is not always effective and may be risky. Going for prolonged periods of time without eating can cause your body to begin storing fat as a response to starvation.

According to Dr. Mattson's study, it takes two to four weeks for the body to adjust to intermittent fasting. When you are getting used to the new schedule, you might feel hungry or irritable. However, he states that research participants who make it past the adjustment period are more likely to stick to the schedule because they feel the benefits.

1.2 Best food choices while following intermittent fasting

Water and zero-calorie drinks, including tea and black coffee, are allowed when you aren't consuming them. And "eating normally" during your eating periods does not suggest "going insane." If you fill your meals with high-calorie fast food, super-sized fried foods, and desserts, you are not going to drop weight or get healthy. Although what most nutritionists love about intermittent fasting is that it helps people eat and enjoy a wide variety of foods. Dr. Williams said, "We want people to be aware and enjoy consuming fresh, healthy food." Eating with others and enjoying the mealtime moment, she continues, adds pleasure, and promotes good health. When you choose complex, unrefined carbs like leafy greens, whole grains, healthy fats, and lean protein, you cannot go wrong.

The foods mentioned below are some of the healthiest you should include in your eating habits when following intermittent fasting.

The Intermittent fasting food list for protein includes:

- Eggs
- Fish and poultry
- Seafood
- Seeds and nuts
- Dairy products such as yogurt, cheese, and milk
- Soy
- Legumes and beans

- Whole grains

The Intermittent food list for carbs includes:

- Bananas
- Brown rice
- Mangoes
- Berries
- Apples
- Kidney beans
- Avocado
- Carrots
- Brussels sprouts
- Broccoli
- Chia seeds
- Almonds
- Chickpeas

The Intermittent fasting food list for fats includes:

- Nuts
- Avocados
- Cheese
- Dark chocolate
- Whole eggs
- Fatty fish
- Extra virgin olive oil (EVOO)
- Chia seeds
- Full-fat yogurt

The Intermittent fasting food list for hydration includes:

- Sparkling water
- Water
- Black coffee or tea
- Plain yogurt
- Watermelon
- Cantaloupe
- Strawberries
- Peaches
- Skim milk

- Oranges
- Cucumber
- Lettuce
- Celery
- Tomatoes

1.3 Is intermittent fasting safe?

Intermittent fasting is a good option compared to long periods of fasting. This entails consuming zero or very few calories for a specified period, followed by eating normally for another set period. The 5:2 diet, for example, involves eating a normal diet for 5 days of the week and consuming a quarter of one's total calories on the other two days. Intermittent fasting and a low-calorie diet were similarly effective for weight reduction and lowering the risk of cancer, cardiac disease, and diabetes, in a report comparing the two methods. Intermittent fasting was discovered to be as easy to adopt as a low-calorie diet.

According to research focused on mouse and rat studies, fasting may protect against some diseases, like diabetes, and can delay aging. In patients being tested for blocked arteries, fasting for brief amounts of time has been linked to a lower BMI, lower rates of diabetes, and a lower risk of coronary artery disease. While limited studies have found a beneficial effect on body weight, blood pressure, and improved rheumatoid arthritis symptoms, there have been no large-scale human studies on fasting. Fasting may be risky to many people's immune systems, but people can obtain medical care when deciding whether or not to fast from time to time. Some people use intermittent fasting to lose weight, and others use it to treat chronic illnesses, including irritable bowel syndrome, elevated cholesterol, or arthritis. But intermittent fasting isn't for everyone.

Before attempting intermittent fasting (or another diet), researchers recommend consulting with your primary care doctor. Some individuals should avoid introducing intermittent fasting to their lifestyle. These include:

- Children and teenagers under the age of 18.
- Women who are expecting a child or who are breastfeeding.
- People who have diabetes or other blood sugar concerns.
- Those who have had an eating disorder in the past.

People who aren't in these groups can successfully perform intermittent fasting and continue the program for as long as they desire. It has the potential to be a lifestyle improvement that brings you many advantages. Keep in your mind that intermittent fasting may also have a variety of consequences depending on the person. If you have unusual distress, headaches, nausea, or any other symptoms after beginning intermittent fasting, consult your doctor.

1.4 Benefits of Intermittent Fasting

Intermittent fasting does more than burn fat, according to research. "Changes in this metabolic switch influence the body and the brain," Dr. Mattson says. Mattson's study was reported in the New England Journal of Medicine, and it revealed information on several health advantages related to the practice. A leaner body, longer life, and a stronger mind are among them. "During intermittent fasting, several things happen that defend organs from chronic diseases such as diabetes, heart failure, age-related neurodegenerative conditions, including inflammatory bowel disease and several cancers," he adds.

Here are some benefits of intermittent fasting that have been discovered so far in research:

Thinking and memory: Intermittent fasting improves working memory in dogs and verbal memory in adults, according to research.

Heart health: Fasting over a short period of time improved resting heart rates, blood pressure, and other heart-related measurements.

Physical performance: Fasting for 16 hours resulted in weight reduction while maintaining muscle mass in young males. Mice that were fed on alternate days had greater running stamina.

Tissue health: Intermittent fasting in animals reduced tissue injury during surgery and improved outcomes.

Obesity and Diabetes: Intermittent fasting has been found to prevent obesity in animals. In six small trials, obese adult humans shed weight by fasting intermittently. So intermittent fasting is also beneficial for humans as well.

Fasting has a lot of advantages, and fat loss isn't one of them. Intermittent fasting has a slew of advantages, including the following.

1. Intermittent fasting can make your day simpler.

Usually, an individual focus on simplicity, behavior change, and reducing stress. Intermittent fasting brings a degree of ease to a diet that you can love. You do not care about breakfast until you wake up. You take a sip of water and begin your day. You like to eat and do not mind preparing, so three meals each day was never a concern for you. However, Intermittent fasting helps you consume one less meal, which ensures you will have to plan one less, cook one less, and worry about one less meal. It makes things a little easier, something you would probably like.

2. Intermittent fasting is the code of longevity.

Scientists understand that eliminating calories will help you live longer. This makes sense from a conceptual perspective. If you are hungry, your body will find ways to improve your life. But there's a problem: who wishes to starve themselves to live longer? A person always wishes to live a long, healthy life. However, it does not seem appealing to starve yourself. The positive news is that intermittent fasting stimulates several of the same pathways that calorie restriction does in prolonging life.

To put it another way, you get the perks of living a longer life without any of the hassles of going hungry. It was discovered in 1945 that intermittent fasting increased the lifespan of mice. More recently, this research discovered intermittent fasting on consecutive days resulted in longer lifespans in humans as well.

3. Intermittent fasting can reduce the risk of cancer.

Since there hasn't been much study and experimentation on the relationship between cancer and fasting, this one is up for discussion. Early indications, on the other hand, are promising. According to a study of ten cancer patients, fasting before treatment may minimize the side effects of chemotherapy. Another research confirms this claim, one that used alternate day fasting for cancer patients and found that fasting before chemotherapy resulted in higher cure rates and fewer deaths. Finally, the analysis of various research on fasting and disease results in the finding that fasting tends to decrease cancer and cardiovascular disease risk.

4. Intermittent fasting is much easier than other diet plans.

Most diets fail not because we turn to the wrong items, but because we do not stick to the diet long enough. It is not a nutrition issue; it is a problem with changing one's habits. This is where intermittent fasting starts because, after you get over the misconception that you ought to eat all the time, it is surprisingly simple to adopt. One research, for example, discovered that intermittent fasting was a successful weight-loss technique in obese people, concluding that "participants rapidly adapt" to an intermittent fasting regimen.

On the contrary between trying a diet plan and trying intermittent fasting, I would like to quote Dr. Michael Eades below, who has attempted intermittent fasting himself.

"Diets are easy to think about but challenging to obey. Intermittent fasting is the exact opposite: it is difficult to consider yet simple to implement. Most people have discussed being on a diet. When we find a diet that relates to us, it seems that following it would be easy. However, as we get down to the details, it gets difficult. E.g., I almost always eat a low-carbohydrate diet. However, if I consider going on a low–fat diet, it seems to be easy. Bagels, whole wheat bread and jam, corn, mashed potatoes, bananas by the dozen, and other foods come to mind, many of which sound delicious. However, if I had to begin a low–fat diet, I would quickly become bored and wish I could enjoy meat and eggs. So, though contemplating a diet is easy, putting one into action over time is more difficult.

There is no way that intermittent fasting is difficult to consider. When we discussed what we were doing, people were shocked and replied, "You go without eating for 24 hours?" "I'd never be prepared to do that." However, once you get underway, it is a snap. For one or two of the three meals a day, you won't have to worry about what to eat or when to eat it. It is a wonderful feeling of liberation. Your food costs drop dramatically. And you are not mostly feeling hungry. While it is difficult to conquer the fear of going without food, nothing could be simpler once you get started."

— Dr. Michael Eades

Eventually, the convenience of intermittent fasting is the greatest motivation to pursue it. It offers a full variety of health benefits without involving a significant change in your lifestyle.

CHAPTER 2: METHODS OF INTERMITTENT FASTING

Fasting, or the restriction of or abstinence from eating food, has been practiced for moral and health reasons since ancient times. Fasting has a long tradition, but it has recently gained popularity as a weight-loss method. There is no such thing as a one-size-fits-all approach to dieting. This is true for intermittent fasting as well. The most important thing is to choose a regimen that suits your lifestyle, fitness, and goals—something that you will continue over time. Women can, in general, take a more casual approach to fast than men. Shorter fasting times, fewer fasting days, and eating a limited number of calories on specific fasting days are possible options. If you're thinking of giving fasting a chance, you have a few choices for integrating it into your everyday routine. In this chapter, we'll go through some of the more common types of fasting and why they're good for both men and women.

Intermittent fasting is most commonly practiced in the following ways:

- The 16/8 method, also called a lean gains method
- Eat-stop-eat, the 24-hour fast once or twice a week
- The 5:2 diet also called a Fast diet
- Random meal skipping method
- Crescendo method, a 12-16 hours or 2-3 days a week fasting method
- Warrior diet
- Alternate day fasting

2.1 The 16/8 method

Daily Intermittent Fasting is another phrase for this specific method. You can follow the Lean Gains intermittent fasting method, which involves a 16–hour fast accompanied by an 8–hour eating cycle. Martin Berkhan of Leangains.com popularized this intermittent daily fasting style, which is where the name comes from.

It makes no difference as to when you start the eight-hour eating period. You will begin at 8 a.m. and end at 4 p.m. alternatively; you could begin at 2 p.m. and finish at 10 p.m. What works for you is what you should adhere to. Eating between 1 and 8 p.m. could be preferable for you because it can allow you to have lunch and dinner with friends and relatives. After all, breakfast is a meal you normally consume alone, so missing it isn't a big deal.

THE 16/8 METHOD

	DAY 1	DAY 2	DAY 3	DAY 4	DAY 5	DAY 6	DAY 7
Midnight 4 AM 8 AM	FAST	FAST	FAST	FAST	FAST	FAST	FAST
12 PM	First meal	First meal	First meal	First meal	First meal	First meal	First meal
4 PM	Last meal by 8pm	Last meal by 8pm	Last meal by 8pm	Last meal by 8pm	Last meal by 8pm	Last meal by 8pm	Last meal by 8pm
8 PM Midnight	FAST	FAST	FAST	FAST	FAST	FAST	FAST

It's very simple to get into the routine of eating on this timetable when regular intermittent fasting is practiced daily. You're probably eating at the same time every day right now without even realizing it. It's the same thing with intermittent daily fasting; you learn not to eat at some hours, which is shockingly easy.

A possible drawback to this schedule is that getting the same number of calories during the week becomes more difficult when you usually skip a meal or two during the day. Simply put, it's hard to teach yourself to consume larger meals regularly. As a consequence, many people who deal with this form of intermittent fasting lose weight. Depending on the priorities, this may be a positive or negative aspect.

This is also a safe time to find out that, while you have been practicing intermittent fasting for the past year, you are not a diet zealot. You primarily focus on developing healthy habits that control your actions 90% of the time so that you can do anything you want with the remaining 10%.

2.2 The 5/2 method

This is one of the most famous fasting practices. The 5:2 fasting system encourages you to eat regularly for five days before limiting your calorie consumption to 500-600 calories for the remaining two. This fasting approach is very adaptable; you can fast for two days of your choice. However, at least one of the non-fasting days should be included between the two.

THE 5:2 METHOD

DAY 1	DAY 2	DAY 3	DAY 4	DAY 5	DAY 6	DAY 7
Eat Normally	Women: 500 Calories Men: 600 Calories	Eat Normally	Eat Normally	Women: 500 Calories Men: 600 Calories	Eat Normally	Eat Normally

The 500 to 600 calories may be eaten in one meal or spread out throughout various meals during the day. Women who consume two meals per day should restrict themselves to 250 calories each meal, and men must limit themselves to 300 calories per meal. This method is simple to obey, particularly if you realize you are less physically active two days a week, which means you'll need to eat fewer calories for energy. When performed correctly, the 5:2 diet can be quite good for weight loss. This is due to the 5:2 eating pattern's ability to make you consume fewer calories. As a result, it is important not to overeat on non-fasting days to compensate for the fasting days.

2.3 Alternate day fasting

This diet, as the name implies, helps you to consume any other day. On Monday, for example, you will eat between the hours of 7-8 a.m. and 7-8 p.m., then fast on a Monday night and the entire day and night on Tuesday. You'd start eating again on Wednesday from 7-8 a.m., in the same order as before.

On fasting days, anyone that uses this approach can consume nutritious foods; on non-fasting days, they should eat anything they choose. This "mix-up" isn't for everybody, but it has its logic. It's better to set out time for yourself because you realize you'll be able to reward yourself afterward. Alternate day intermittent fasting requires fasting for prolonged stretches on various days of the week.

You will, for example, eat dinner on a Monday night, and then you will not eat again until Tuesday evening as shown in the graphic below. You will feed all day on Wednesday, then resume the 24-hour fasting period after dinner on Wednesday evening. This helps you to sustain long fast cycles while also consuming at least one meal per day of the week.

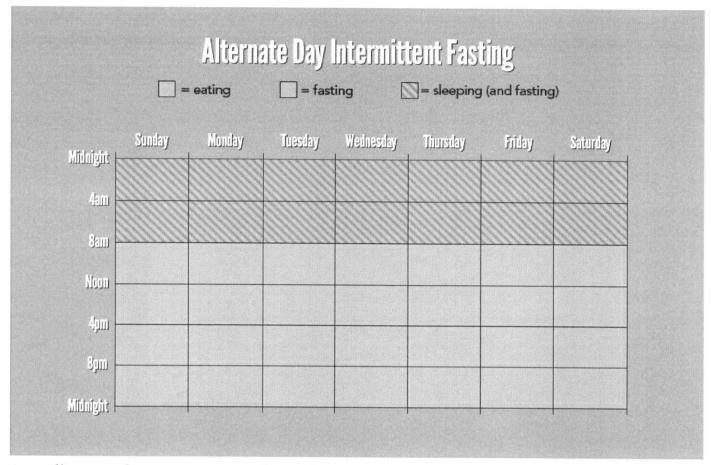

According to what most surveys have shown, this intermittent fasting method tends to be common in clinical studies, but it isn't very common in the real world. Alternate-day intermittent fasting has the advantage of allowing you more days in the fasted state than the Lean Gains process. This, in practice, would boost the effects of fasting. Hypothetically, however, you might be nervous about not eating enough. One of the most difficult aspects of intermittent fasting is teaching yourself to consume more constantly. You may be able to feast for a meal, but it requires a little planning, a lot of preparation, and consistent cooking to do so every day of the week. Consequently, most people who attempt intermittent fasting lose weight while the size of their meals stays consistent even though a few meals are skipped per week.

This isn't a concern if you're attempting to lose weight. And if you're comfortable with your weight, following the regular or weekly fasting routines won't be too difficult. However, if you fast for 24 hours a day on several days a week, it would be extremely difficult to consume sufficiently on your feast days to compensate. Consequently, most nutritionists agree that attempting regular intermittent fasting or a single 24-hour fast once a week or once a month is a safer option.

2.4 The warrior diet

Ori Hofmekler, a former participant of the Israeli Special Forces who moved into health and fitness, developed the Warrior Diet in 2001. This diet is a form of intermittent fasting, which is an umbrella term for eating habits that involve cycles of low-calorie consumption for a fixed period. The Warrior Diet is focused on ancient warriors' dietary habits, which consisted of eating nothing throughout the day and only feasting at night. The Warrior Diet is a form of eating that alternates lengthy stretches of eating less with brief periods of eating a lot. It has been promoted as a good way to lose weight, increase stamina, and gain mental clarity. A 20-hour fast is thought to be one of the old fasting methods.

THE WARRIOR DIET

	DAY 1	DAY 2	DAY 3	DAY 4	DAY 5	DAY 6	DAY 7
Midnight 4 AM 8 AM 12 PM	Eating only small amounts of vegetables and fruits	Eating only small amounts of vegetables and fruits	Eating only small amounts of vegetables and fruits	Eating only small amounts of vegetables and fruits	Eating only small amounts of vegetables and fruits	Eating only small amounts of vegetables and fruits	Eating only small amounts of vegetables and fruits
4 PM	Large meal	Large meal	Large meal	Large meal	Large meal	Large meal	Large meal
8 PM Midnight							

This method encourages you to consume small portions of particular foods at dinner. You can also work out during dinner time. You'd have an eating window at the end of the day. While this approach is difficult to adopt, it is extremely convenient and yields incredible results. Few people choose to do so for a week or two before a big event or a photo session, but few people have the willpower to stick to it for prolonged periods. Remember that you don't have to push yourself to stick to an extreme eating schedule if it leaves you hungry and tired; pick the one that is more manageable and easier to follow!

2.5 Eat-stop-eat

A 24-hour fast is described as going without food from breakfast to breakfast, lunch to lunch, or dinner to dinner, whichever you choose. If you consume dinner at 7 p.m. on Day 1, for example, you can fast before 7 p.m. on Day 2. You may not have to fast for 24 hours, despite what the title says. You should eat one meal to tide you over and use the time to take supplements that need to be taken with meals. It is not for everybody, much like The Warrior Diet is not for everybody. If you really need to lose weight quickly, you can follow this fasting approach for a limited amount of time because it provides excellent results. It may be the day before your wedding or the day after a big Thanksgiving or Christmas meal that leaves you feeling bloated. But be smart and pay attention to your body! Moving from a complete day of feasting to a 24-hour fast can be incredibly stressful on the body. Weight reduction is one of the primary motivations for people to try intermittent fasting regimes like the Eat Stop Eat method.

EAT-STOP-EAT

DAY 1	DAY 2	DAY 3	DAY 4	DAY 5	DAY 6	DAY 7
Eats normally	24-hour fast	Eats normally	Eats normally	24-hour fast	Eats normally	Eats normally

While there are currently no studies testing Eat Stop Eat for weight loss, mounting evidence indicates that the intermittent, prolonged fasting used by Eat Stop Eat can aid many people with losing weight. Moreover, a calorie deficiency is the first and maybe the most noticeable way Eat Stop Eat will help you lose weight. It's popular knowledge that dropping weight necessitates eating fewer calories than you burn. Eat Stop Eat, when used right, sets you up with a calorie loss of 1–2 days per week. This decrease in total calorie intake will result in weight loss over time as you burn more calories than you consume.

2.6 Spontaneous meal skipping

The emphasis of random meal skipping is mostly on consuming unprocessed foods. Besides that, fasting rules are rather adjustable, and you can miss meals once or twice a week at random. Spontaneous meal skipping is a practice of listening to the body. It states that if your body does not indicate that you are hungry, you do not have to eat. The theory behind Spontaneous meal skipping is to respond to your body's cues. It supports the idea that rather than overloading your body with food excessively, even though you aren't starving, you can allow your body a pause for some time.

SPONTANEOUS MEAL SKIPPING

	DAY 1	DAY 2	DAY 3	DAY 4	DAY 5	DAY 6	DAY 7
	Breakfast	Skipped Meal	Breakfast	Breakfast	Breakfast	Breakfast	Breakfast
	Lunch	Lunch	Lunch	Lunch	Lunch	Lunch	Lunch
	Dinner	Dinner	Dinner	Dinner	Skipped Meal	Dinner	Dinner

This fasting method is ideal for busy people and those who have little time to practice various diets. It essentially assists you in reducing your calorie consumption. If you had a very heavy lunch, you might want to give your body a break and miss dinner, or at the very least eat something light, but don't overeat as you take the next meal after missing a meal. It has the potential to induce negative shifts in your body's metabolic function, which is harmful to your health. So, during your meal, make sure you consume in moderation. Make no effort to cover for the missing meal. Eat like you normally would.

2.7 Crescendo Fasting

If you're a woman, you've already heard that men have an easier time losing weight than women do. For us women, this can be frustrating! Hormone imbalances can render weight reduction difficult. If you're starving yourself regularly with intermittent fasting (IF), you'll become tired and ravenous and will end up eating whatever you can get your hands on. Your body will even begin to break down your lean muscle for fuel rather than fat. So crescendo fasting is perhaps the most beginner-friendly way of fasting.

Contrary to common belief, crescendo fasting operates gently with hormones to create a balanced equilibrium, helping you maintain your appetite and stamina while still losing body fat. Fasting can occur but in shorter, less regular bursts. This is a healthy approach to reducing your calorie intake and losing weight without putting your body in a stressful deprivation mode. After a while, you might feel more at ease fasting for longer and more regular periods. Instead of the standard IF protocol, which may have you fasting anytime from 12 to 20 hours a day, crescendo fasting reduces the fasting period to only two to three non-consecutive days a week. The word "crescendo fasting" accurately explains its goal: steadily increasing the amount of fasting the body can tolerate. So, for example, you might fast for 14 hours, beginning at 9 p.m. on Sunday and finishing at 11 a.m. on Monday. After that, you'll normally eat for the next few days before repeating the fast. It's easy and incredibly simple to execute. It often relieves a lot of anxiety if you have problems doing intermittent fasting regularly. Additionally, the body will be able to respond to longer fasts over time, allowing you to adopt a more conventional intermittent fasting schedule.

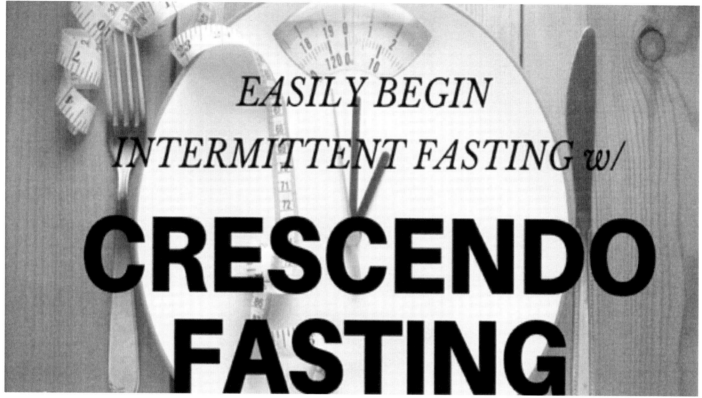

This is a simplified edition of the 16-8 technique. You choose two to three days a week to fast for 12-16 hours. The Crescendo Method is one that can be interpreted in a variety of ways. Some people believe you can fast for 12 waking hours, and others believe you should fast for a total of 16 hours. The Crescendo Method is usually used as a stepping stone into the Eat-Fast-Eat Method. Begin by fasting for 12 hours twice a week and gradually increase to 24 hours.

12-hour fast:

A 12-hour fast is described as eating for the first 12 hours of the day and then not eating for the next 12 hours. If you consume three meals a day between 8 a.m. and 8 p.m., for example, you can fast from 8 p.m. to 8 a.m. This approach is simple to execute and yields excellent outcomes in the long term.

Even though it is claimed that your body runs out of blood sugar eight hours after the last meal. It ensures that if you fast for 12 hours, you would only be burning fat for 4 hours. Of course, that's better than nothing, but keep in mind that you should start with this one, check your progress, and gradually increase your fasting period before you're able to implement the 16:8 method!

16-hour fast:

Fasting for 16 hours is a little more difficult than 12 hours, but the effects are much better. As the name suggests, you can fast for 16 hours and then eat for the remaining 8 hours of the day. While fasting this way, you must eat a lot of high-protein items and rotate your carbohydrate intake. If you work out, you can try to plan your nutrient intake carefully. This ensures that you can eat the rest of the carbs right after a workout. When you eat from 11 a.m. to 7 p.m., for example, you can eat two or four to five meals during that time and fast from 7 p.m. to 11 a.m. Any people who fast this way tend to miss the morning meal every day and still eat snacks before their other meals. This is currently the most common fasting form, and it has the best ease-of-follow and efficacy ratio!

At the end of the day, the perfect approach is something that you can handle and maintain over time without causing any negative health effects.

CHAPTER 3: INTERMITTENT FASTING FOR WOMEN OVER 50

Intermittent Fasting may affect women and men differently. According to some reports, intermittent fasting might not be as effective for some women as it is for men. In one research, women's blood sugar regulation decreased after 3 weeks of intermittent fasting, while men's blood sugar control improved. There have also been several observational accounts about women's menstrual cycles shifting since they started intermittent fasting, since female bodies are particularly vulnerable to calorie restriction, such shifts may arise. A small portion of the brain, known as the hypothalamus, is impaired when calorie consumption is limited, such as when fasting for too long or too often. Gonadotropin-releasing hormone (GnRH) is a hormone that aids in the activation of two sex hormones: follicle-stimulating hormone (FSH) and luteinizing hormone (LH). When these hormones cannot interact with the ovaries, irregular cycles, miscarriage, poor bone strength, and other health problems may occur. While no equivalent human trials exist, 3–6 months of alternate-day fasting in female rats resulted in decreased ovary size and irregular menstrual cycles. So, women should take a modified solution to intermittent fasting, like shorter fasting times and fewer fasting days, due to these factors. As a consequence, it is advisable that you take medical guidance and consult your doctor before starting any diet.

3.1 How To Start Intermittent Fasting?

It is simple to get started. In reality, you have probably done a few intermittent fasts before. Often people eat this way out of habit, avoiding breakfast and dinner. The most straightforward approach to get started is to use one of the intermittent fasting plans listed above. You may not, though, have to stick to a strict schedule. Another choice is to fast anytime it is convenient for you. For certain individuals, skipping meals because they are not hungry or do not have time to prepare may be beneficial. It does not matter the kind of fast you want at the end of the day. Finding a tool that fits well for you and your lifestyle is the most important thing.

It is important to remember that intermittent fasting is not a diet. It is a method of eating that is scheduled. Intermittent fasting, unlike a dietary schedule that restricts where calories come from, does not prescribe which foods an individual should consume or avoid. The following tips are intended to assist women or men who are ready to begin fasting and make it as convenient and successful as possible.

1. Identify your personal goals:

An individual who begins intermittent fasting usually has a specific target in mind. That may be for weight loss, better physical health, or better metabolic function. A person's ultimate goal can help them decide on the right fasting approach and measure how many nutrients and calories they need.

2. Pick up the right method:

Before undertaking another fasting method, a person can typically stay with one for at least a month. When it comes to fasting for health benefits, there are four options to consider. Women should select the plan that better fits their needs and the one they feel they will stick to. These include:

- The 16/8 method
- The 5:2 diet
- Alternate day fasting
- Eat stop eat
- The warrior diets
- Spontaneous meal skipping
- Crescendo fasting

3. Figure out the caloric needs:

When fasting, while there are no food limits, calories must always be counted. People who choose to lose weight would build a calorie deficit, which implies they must gain fewer calories than they consume. Many that wish to add weight would eat more calories than they spend. There are various resources available to help individuals estimate their caloric requirements and decide how many calories they must eat per day to maintain or lose weight. An individual may also seek advice from a healthcare professional or a dietitian on how many calories they require while following intermittent fasting.

4. Figure out a meal plan:

Making a weekly meal schedule will assist anyone who is seeking to reduce or gain weight. A woman attempting to lose weight with intermittent fasting may find that preparing their meals for the day or week is helpful. Meal preparation does not have to be restrictive. It considers calorie consumption and ensures that the correct foods are used in the diet. Meal prep has many advantages, including assisting with calorie counting and ensuring that an individual has the necessary ingredients on hand for preparing foods, fast dinners, and snacks.

5. Make the calories count:

Calories are not always made equal. Since these intermittent fasting methods do not specify how many calories an individual can ingest when fasting, it's important that the food's nutritional content is considered. In general, nutrient-dense food, or food with many nutrients per calorie, should be consumed. Even if individuals do not have to avoid fast food completely, they can also consume it in moderation and concentrate on healthy alternatives to enjoy the most benefits.3.2 Some Dietary Requirements With Age

As we get older, our nutritional requirements change, and eating healthy becomes more important. Since aging is related to various changes, particularly nutrient deficiencies, lower quality of life, and poor health results, this is the case. Fortunately, you should take measures to help avoid weaknesses and other age-related shifts. Eating nutrient-dense diets and getting the right supplements, for example, will help you remain healthier as you grow older. This chapter discusses how the dietary requirements shift when you get older and how to satisfy them.

How Does Aging Affect the Nutritional Needs?

Several body changes are associated with aging, including

muscle weakness, thinner skin, and lower stomach acid. As you get older, your ability to recognize hunger and thirst can deteriorate. Any of these shifts can put you at risk for nutritional shortages, while others may affect the senses and overall quality of life. According to research, 20% of older adults suffer from atrophic gastritis, a disorder in which chronic inflammation damages the cells that contain stomach acid. Low stomach acid may prevent nutrients like vitamin B12, iron, calcium, and magnesium from being absorbed.

Another issue that arises as people age is a decrease in their calorie requirements. Unfortunately, this results in a nutritional dilemma. Although consuming fewer calories, older adults need almost as much, if not more, of those nutrients. Fortunately, you may satisfy your nutritional requirements by consuming a range of whole foods and taking supplements. Another problem that people may face when they grow older is a decline in their body's ability to recognize essential senses such as hunger and thirst. Unintended weight loss and dehydration can happen as a result of this. And as you grow older, these effects can get more severe.

Needing fewer calories, but more nutrients:

The daily calorie requirements of a person are defined by their activity level, weight, height, muscle mass, and several other variables. In general, older adults require fewer calories. However, their nutritional requirements remain the same as, or higher than when they were younger. As a result, consuming nutrient-dense, whole foods becomes important. Since they walk and work out less and carry less muscle, older adults need fewer calories to sustain their weight. If you proceed to consume the same number of calories every day as you did when you were young, you are likely to gain weight, especially around your abdomen. This is especially true of postmenopausal women, as the decrease in estrogen levels during this period can stimulate the storage of belly fat.

Even if older adults need fewer calories, they still need the same or even higher amounts of nutrients than younger people. This highlights the value of consuming a range of whole foods, such as vegetables, fruits, fish, and lean meats, for older people. These nutrient-dense foods will help you combat nutrient deficiency without adding inches to your waistline. Protein, calcium, vitamin D, and vitamin B12 are all nutrients that become more necessary when you grow older.

You can benefit from more protein:

As you get older, it is normal to lose muscle and energy. In reality, after the age of 30, the average person loses 3–8% of their muscle mass per decade. Sarcopenia is the term for lack of muscle mass and strength. It is a leading cause of elderly weakness, injuries, and poor health. More protein in your diet can help your body retain muscle mass and combat sarcopenia.

Over the span of three years, a survey observed 2,066 elderly citizens. It was discovered that those who consumed the most protein a day lost 40% less muscle mass than those who ate the least. A study of 20 recent research in older adults showed that increasing protein consumption or getting protein supplements would increase muscle mass, delay muscle loss, and improve muscle growth. Furthermore, the most successful approach to combat sarcopenia seems to be balancing a protein-rich diet with resistance exercise.

You may benefit from more fiber:

Constipation is a major health issue among older people. It is more prevalent among people over the age of 65, and women are two or three times more likely to suffer from it than men. This is because individuals in their forties and fifties appear to walk less and are more prone to take pills with constipation as a side effect. Constipation may be relieved by eating fiber. It flows through the intestines undigested, assisting in the formation of stool and the maintenance of normal bowel movements. Dietary fiber helped trigger bowel movements in individuals with constipation, according to a study of five reports.

Diverticular disease is a disorder in which tiny pouches develop along the colon wall and become inflamed or infected. A high-fiber diet can help avoid this. This is a particularly frequent ailment among the elderly. Diverticular disease is sometimes mistaken as a disease induced by a Western diet. It is very common, with up to 50% of citizens over the age of 50 in Western countries suffering from it. However, Diverticular disease is nearly non-existent in people who consume more fiber. Diverticular disorder, for example, affects fewer than 0.2 percent of the population in Japan and Africa. Increasing your fiber consumption will help you protect yourself from both this disease and constipation.

You need more vitamin D and calcium:

Two of the most essential minerals for bone protection are calcium and vitamin D. When you grow older, the body can benefit from more vitamin D and calcium. Calcium aids in the formation and maintenance of healthy bones, whereas vitamin D aids in calcium absorption. Unfortunately, older adults have a lower ability to digest calcium from their food. According to animal and human research, the gut consumes less calcium the more we age.

However, since aging will make the body less effective at producing vitamin D, the decrease in calcium absorption is more likely due to a vitamin D deficiency. When your skin is exposed to sunlight, your body will generate vitamin D from the skin's cholesterol. However, when people age, their skin becomes thinner, reducing their capacity to produce vitamin D. These shifts can prevent you from having enough vitamin D and calcium, leading to bone loss and an increased risk of fracture. It is necessary to eat more calcium and vitamin D from foods and supplements to combat the impact of aging on vitamin D and calcium levels. Calcium is found in a variety of foods, including dark green, leafy vegetables, and animal products. On the other hand, Vitamin D could be present in several kinds of seafood, including herring and salmon. Vitamin D supplements, such as cod liver oil, may also help older people.

You may need more vitamin B12:

Vitamin B12, commonly known as cobalamin, is a water-soluble vitamin. Vitamin B12 deficiency is more common as people become older. Having a vitamin B12 supplement or eating foods enriched with vitamin B12 may be particularly beneficial to older adults. It is needed for the production of red blood cells as well as the maintenance of normal brain function. Unfortunately, studies show that 10–30% of adults over the age of 50 have a reduced ability to consume vitamin B12 from food, leading to a vitamin B12 imbalance. Vitamin B12 is bound to proteins in the foods you consume in your diet. Stomach acid will help it detach from such food proteins so the body can use it.

In older persons, disorders that decrease stomach acid output are more common, resulting in lower vitamin B12 absorption from food. One disease that may do this is atrophic gastritis. Furthermore, since vitamin B12 is more plentiful in animal foods like eggs, seafood, meat, and dairy, older persons who adopt a vegetarian or vegan diet are less likely to obtain high-quality vitamin sources. As a result, older people can benefit from getting a vitamin B12 supplement or eating vitamin B12-fortified foods. The crystalline vitamin B12 in these fortified foods is not bound to food proteins. As a result, individuals who produce lower stomach acid than average are still able to absorb it.

Some other nutrients that may help you as you age:

Other nutrients that could be beneficial when you get older include Magnesium, potassium, omega-3 fatty acids, and iron.

Potassium: A higher potassium consumption is linked to a reduced risk of elevated blood pressure, osteoporosis, kidney stones, and cardiac failure, all of which are more prevalent in older people.

Omega-3 fatty acids: The main cause of death in the elderly is heart failure. Omega-3 fatty acids have been shown in studies to reduce cardiac attack risk factors such as triglycerides and elevated blood pressure. Fish is the primary provider of omega-3 fats.

Magnesium: Magnesium is an essential mineral for the human body. Unfortunately, due to medication use, inadequate intake, and age-related gut function changes, older people are at risk of deficiency.

Iron: Iron deficiency is common in the older population. Anemia, a disorder in which the blood does not provide enough oxygen to the bloodstream, can occur due to this. A diet rich in vegetables, fruits, seafood, and lean meats will provide most of these nutrients. People who follow a vegetarian or vegan diet, on the other hand, can benefit from having omega-3 or an iron supplement. While iron can be present in many vegetables, plant-based iron is not as well absorbed as meat-based iron.

You are more prone to dehydration:

Drinking lots of water becomes more important as you grow older because your body can lose the potential to recognize dehydration. Water takes up around 60% of the body. It is important to remain hydrated at any age because the body loses water regularly, mostly through sweat and urine. Additionally, when you get older, you can become more vulnerable to dehydration. Thirst is detected by receptors located in the brain and all over the body. These can become less receptive to water changes as you age, making it more difficult for them to sense thirst. Your kidneys still help your body store water, but they also start to lose function as you get older.

Sad to say, but dehydration has serious effects on aged people. Long-term dehydration reduces the fluid in the cells, making it harder to digest medicine, causing health issues and growing fatigue. As a result, it is important to make a deliberate attempt to consume enough water regularly. If you have issues drinking water, consider getting one or two glasses with each meal. Otherwise, take a water bottle with you during the day.

You may struggle to eat enough food:

Another point of concern for the aged is a lack of appetite. If this dilemma is not solved, it may result in unwanted weight loss and dietary deficiencies. Appetite deficiency has also been related to a higher risk of mortality or poor health. Changes in taste and smell, hormones, and changes in life conditions may all contribute to a loss of appetite in older adults. According to research, older people have higher levels of fullness hormones and lower levels of hunger hormones, suggesting they may eat less often and feel fuller sooner. Researchers also noticed in a small study of 11 aged persons and 11 young adults, that older adults have slightly lower amounts of the appetite hormone ghrelin before a meal.

Furthermore, numerous experiments have reported that the fullness hormones leptin and cholecystokinin are higher in older people. Aging will impair the sense of taste and smell, leaving foods less appealing. Tooth loss, underlying illness, loneliness, and appetite-suppressing medications are also possible causes of poor appetite. If eating big meals is tough for you, consider splitting your meals into smaller pieces and eating them every few hours. Otherwise, continue and make a routine of snacking on healthy foods, including yogurt, nuts, and boiled eggs, which are high in nutrients and calories.

3.3 Health Benefits of Intermittent fasting for women

Intermittent fasting is an eating practice in which a person only eats during a specific amount of time. The 16/8 process, in which you eat for 8 hours and then fast for 16, is the most common form of intermittent fasting. Intermittent fasting has been proven to help people lose weight in several research reports. Furthermore, several test-tube and animal researches indicated that intermittent fasting can help older people by extending life, preventing age-related changes in mitochondria, and slowing cell decline, the cell's energy-producing organelles. Intermittent fasting will help you lose weight while still lowering the risk of developing various chronic diseases.

Heart Health

The main cause of death in the world is heart failure. High

blood pressure, high triglyceride levels, and high LDL cholesterol are the three most common risk factors for cardiac failure. In a study of 16 obese men and women, intermittent fasting reduced blood pressure by 6% in only eight weeks. According to the same report, intermittent fasting also cut triglycerides by 32%, and LDL cholesterol by 25%. The evidence for a correlation between intermittent fasting and lower LDL triglyceride levels and cholesterol, on the other hand, is inconsistent.

Four weeks of intermittent fasting over the Islamic holidays of Ramadan did not result in a decrease in LDL cholesterol or triglycerides, according to a survey of 40 normal-weight individuals. Before researchers fully comprehend the impact of intermittent fasting on cardiac health, higher-quality research with more rigorous methods is still needed.

Diabetes

Intermittent fasting will also help you treat your diabetes and lower your risk of developing it. Intermittent fasting, including prolonged calorie restriction, tends to reduce many of the disease's risk factors. It mostly does this by lowering insulin levels and decreasing insulin tolerance.

Six months of intermittent fasting showed decreased insulin levels by 29% and insulin tolerance by 19% in a randomized controlled trial of more than a hundred overweight or obese women. The levels of blood sugar remained unchanged. Furthermore, intermittent fasting for 8–12 weeks has been found to decrease insulin levels by approximately 20–31% and blood glucose levels by 3–6% in people with pre-diabetes, a disease in which blood sugar levels are increased but not elevated enough to diagnose diabetes. In terms of blood sugar, though, intermittent fasting might not be as effective for women as men. A small study showed that women's blood sugar balance deteriorated after twenty-two days of alternate day fasting, although men's blood sugar levels were unaffected. Despite this side effect, the decrease in insulin and insulin tolerance will reduce the probability of diabetes, particularly in pre-diabetic individuals.

Weight Loss

When performed right, intermittent fasting can be an easy and efficient way to reduce weight since short-term fasts will help you eat fewer calories. Several reports have shown that intermittent fasting is just as effective as conventional calorie-restricted diet plans for weight loss in the short term. Intermittent fasting resulted in an overall weight reduction of 15 lbs., approximately 6.8 kg over 3–12 months, according to a 2018 study of research on overweight adults. For 3–24 weeks, intermittent fasting decreased body weight by 3–8% in obese or overweight people, according to another study. According to the report, participants' waist circumference decreased by 3–7% during the same period.

It is important to note that the long-term consequences of intermittent fasting on female weight loss are unknown. Intermittent fasting appears to help with weight reduction in the short term. However, the amount you lose can almost definitely be determined by how many calories you consume during non-fasting hours and how long you stick to the lifestyle.

It May Help You Eat Less

Moving to intermittent fasting may help you eat less naturally. According to one report, when young men's food consumption was limited to a four-hour duration, they consumed 650 fewer calories per day. Another research looked at the impact of a lengthy, 36-hour fast on 24 active men's and women's eating patterns. Despite eating more calories on the post-fast day, participants' overall calorie balance dropped by 1,900 calories, which significantly decreased.

Other Health Benefits

Intermittent fasting can also have a range of other health effects, according to a variety of animal and human reports. These include:

Reduced inflammation: Intermittent fasting has been shown in several trials to suppress key markers of inflammation. Chronic inflammation can induce weight gain and various other health issues.

Improved psychological health: In one report, 8 weeks of intermittent fasting reduced stress and binge eating habits in obese adults, thus improving body image.

Increased longevity: Intermittent fasting was also shown to extend lifespan by 33–83 percent in rats and mice. Fasting causes cells to go through an adaptive stress reaction, explaining why it has so many positive outcomes. Fasting on alternate days increases oxidative stress markers and is an indicator of longevity.

Preserve muscle mass: When compared to prolonged calorie restriction, intermittent fasting tends to be more efficient at maintaining muscle mass. And even when you are at rest, gaining more muscle mass makes you burn more calories. Intermittent fasting is likely to result in more muscle gain than most weight-loss diets. Adding exercise to the intermittent fasting plan, especially weightlifting, will help you retain muscle mass. It is, though, completely up to you whether or not you work out during fasting times.

3.4 When Women Should Not Fast?

Many women tend to remain healthy by using modified forms of intermittent fasting. On the other hand, various studies have shown that fasting days will induce hunger, mood fluctuations, loss of focus, diminished stamina, headaches, and bad breath. According to several reports on the internet, women's menstrual cycles have also been said to have ceased while on an intermittent fasting diet. Before undertaking intermittent fasting, contact the doctor if you have a medical problem. Intermittent fasting is not recommended for the following women:

- Women who have a background of eating disorders should seek medical advice immediately.

- Have diabetes or suffer low blood sugar levels daily. When you have Type 1 diabetes, you have the risk of acquiring excessively elevated blood glucose levels (hyperglycemia), which may lead to a build-up of 'ketones.' Ketoacidosis is a serious condition that may occur as a result of this. Passing a lot of urine, feeling very thirsty, or becoming very sleepy are all signs of elevated blood glucose levels. Speak with a healthcare provider if your blood glucose levels are elevated, and you have these symptoms.

- Are underweight, malnourished, or deficient in nutrients. The fast duration determines the changes that arise in the body during a continuous fast. Eight hours or so after the last meal, your body typically enters a fasting condition. Your body can first use glucose stored in your body, then break down body fat as the next energy source later in the fast. Using your body's fat reserves as an energy supply will result in weight loss in the long term.

- Are breastfeeding, pregnant, or trying to conceive? Fasting or starvation over an extended amount of time when breastfeeding should be ceased because it will limit milk supply, slowing the baby's weight gain over time. According to research, fasting for a short period will not affect your milk supply. And if you are not eating anything, your body can go to considerable lengths to keep producing milk for your baby. But that does not makes fasting a good choice. The nutritional content of a mother's milk is primarily determined by her diet, according to research. You absorb fewer minerals and vitamins overall when you consume fewer calories. As a consequence, milk can become less nutritious in the longer term.

- If you should conceive, IF may not be the perfect lifestyle choice for a fast-growing infant. Pregnancy necessitates a significant number of resources. Women who are pregnant need to consume more calories every day, so trying IF or staying with it during pregnancy can be placed on pause until you can speak to the doctor about it.

- Have experienced fertility issues or a diagnosis of amenorrhea (missed periods.)

That being said, intermittent fasting seems to have a favorable protection profile. However, if you have any complications, such as a lack of your menstrual period, you can quit instantly. Updated versions of intermittent fasting, on the other hand, tend to be healthy for most women and could be a safer choice than longer or tougher fasts. Intermittent fasting is something to think about if you are a woman trying to reduce weight or boost your health.

CHAPTER 4: THE BEST APPROACHES TO LOSE WEIGHT AFTER 50

Maintaining a healthy weight or losing extra body fat will be tough for certain people when they grow older. Weight increase over the age of 50 can be caused by unhealthy habits, a mainly sedentary lifestyle, metabolic shifts, and bad dietary choices. You are capable of losing weight at any age, regardless of your physical abilities or medical diagnoses, by making a few basic changes.

4.1 Some Weight Loss Strategies

Here are the top 19 weight-loss strategies for people over 50.

1. Learn to enjoy strength training.

Strength training is still critical for older adults, even though cardio receives a lot of focus when it comes to losing weight. Sarcopenia is a disorder in which muscle mass reduces when you grow older. At about 50, muscle mass loss begins, which will hinder the metabolism and contribute to weight gain. After 50, your muscle mass declines at a pace of about 12% per year, while your muscle power declines at a rate of 1.5–5% per year. Using muscle-building workouts in your regimen is important for reducing age-related muscle decline and maintaining healthy body weight.

Bodyweight workouts and weightlifting, for example, will boost muscle strength and size while still growing muscle efficiency. Physical exercise will also help you reduce weight by lowering body fat and increasing your metabolism, which will help you burn more calories during the day.

2. Team up.

It may not be easy to develop a balanced eating schedule or workout regimen on your own. Sticking to the schedule and achieving your fitness objectives can be more enjoyable if you team up with a buddy, coworker, or family member. According to studies, people who participate in weight-loss exercises with partners are more likely to keep their weight loss over time. Working out with others will help you stay committed to your fitness regimen and make things more exciting.

3. Move more and sit less.

To lose excess body fat, you must burn more calories than you consume. That is why, when attempting to lose weight, becoming more active during the day is important. Sitting at your desk for long periods, for example, can hinder your weight loss efforts. To combat this, actually getting up from the desk and having a five-minute walk every hour will help you feel more involved at work. According to studies, using a Fitbit or pedometer to watch your steps will help you lose weight by increasing your activity and calorie expenditure. Start with a rational step target focused on the current activity rate by using a pedometer or Fitbit. Then, based on your general fitness, gradually increase from 7,000 to 10,000 steps a day or more.

4. Bump up the protein intake.

It is important to have enough high-quality amount of protein in your diet, not just for weight reduction but also to avoid or reverse age-related muscle loss. After the age of 20, the resting metabolic rate (RMR), or the number of calories you burn at rest, drops by 1–2% per decade. This is linked to muscle weakness as people become older. A protein-rich diet, on the other hand, may help inhibit or even restore muscle loss. Increasing dietary protein has also been shown in several trials to help you shed weight and maintain keeping it off in the long run. Furthermore, evidence suggests that older adults need more protein than young people, emphasizing the importance of including protein-rich items in your snacks and meals.

5. Talk to your dietitian.

It may be challenging to find an eating routine that encourages weight loss while still nourishing the body. A certified dietitian will help you determine the most effective way to remove extra body fat without needing to stick to a strict diet. A dietitian will also help you lose weight by providing advice and guidance. According to studies, getting training with a nutritionist or dietician may achieve far more outcomes and benefits than going it alone, and it can even help you sustain your weight loss over time.

6. Cook more at home.

Numerous tests have shown that those who cook and consume more food at home have a better diet and are less obese than those that do not. When you prepare meals at home, you have complete control of what goes into and what remains out of your recipes. It also allows you to try fresh, healthy ingredients that have piqued your interest. Start by cooking one or two meals at home a week if you eat out most of the time, then gradually increase this amount until you are cooking at home more than you eat out.

7. Eat more fruits and vegetables.

Fruits and vegetables are rich in nutrients that are important for good health, and having them in your diet is an easy, scientifically proven way to lose weight. An analysis of ten research showed that increasing regular vegetable servings are linked to a 0.14-inch (0.36-cm) waist circumference drop in women. Another research found that consuming fruits and vegetables decreased body weight, waist circumference, and body fat in 26,340 women and men aged 35–65.

8. Hire a personal trainer.

Working with a personal trainer can be particularly beneficial for people who are new to working out. They can show you not only how to work out properly and lose weight, but how to avoid injury. Personal trainers will also encourage you to exercise frequently by making you accountable. They could even change your mind about working out. A 10-week survey of 129 adults reported that 1 hour of one-on-one personal training sessions improved fitness motivation and physical activity levels each week.

9. Rely less on convenience foods.

Eating convenience foods like fast food, sweets, and packaged foods regularly have been linked to weight gain and can hinder weight loss efforts. Convenience foods are high in calories and low in essential nutrients such as protein, fiber, and minerals. Fast food and other packaged items are sometimes referred to as "empty calories" because of this. Cutting down on convenience foods and replacing them with nutrient-dense whole foods in healthy meals and snacks is a good way to lose weight and stay healthy.

10. Find an activity that you love.

Finding a workout regimen that you can stick to for the long term could be challenging. This is why it is important to participate in activities you love. Sign up for a community sport like a running club or soccer if you enjoy group sports. This would encourage you to exercise with others daily. If you enjoy solitary workouts, go for a cycle trip, a stroll, a climb, or a swim.

11. Get checked by a healthcare provider.

Suppose you are having difficulty losing weight after being active and maintaining a balanced diet. In that case, you can rule out factors that make it difficult to lose weight, such as polycystic ovarian syndrome (PCOS) and hypothyroidism. This is especially true if you have relatives that suffer from these ailments. Tell the doctor the concerns regarding this, so he or she can determine the right testing procedure to rule out any medical issues that may be causing your weight loss problems.

12. Eat a whole-foods-based diet.

Following a diet abundant in whole grains is one of the best ways to guarantee that the body receives the nutrition it needs to survive. Whole foods, such as vegetables, fruits, seeds, nuts, poultry, seafood, grains, and legumes, are high in fiber, protein, and good fats, all of which are important for maintaining a healthy body weight. Whole-food-based diets, both plant-based and those containing animal products, have been related to weight reduction in various trials.

13. Eat less at night.

Many researchers have found that consuming fewer calories at night will help you sustain a healthier weight and lose unwanted fat. Over six years, those who ingested more calories at dinner were more than twice as likely to become obese than those who ate more calories earlier in the day, according to a survey of 1,245 individuals. Furthermore, people who consumed more calories at dinner were more likely to experience metabolic syndrome, a category of disorders like elevated blood sugar levels and excess belly fat. Diabetes, heart disease, and stroke are all worsened by metabolic syndrome. Breakfast and lunch can provide the bulk of the calories, so a lighter dinner could be a viable choice for weight reduction.

14. Focus on body composition.

While your body weight is a strong indicator of fitness, body composition, including fat and fat-free mass ratios, is also important. Muscle mass, especially in older adults, is a significant predictor of optimal health. Your aim should be to add more muscle while losing weight. There are many approaches for measuring body fat levels. However, measuring the waist, calves, biceps, chest, and thighs will help you find out whether you are losing weight and adding muscle.

15. Stay hydrated in a healthy way.

Drinks with added sugars and calories, such as sweetened coffee beverages, juices, soda, sports drinks, and pre-made smoothies, are common. Sugar-sweetened drinks, particularly those sweetened with high-fructose corn syrup, have been related to weight gain and obesity, cardiac disease, diabetes, and fatty liver disease. Substituting sugary beverages for nutritious drinks like water and herbal tea will help you lose weight and lower the risk of contracting the chronic conditions listed above.

16. Choose the right supplements.

If you are exhausted and unmotivated, the right nutrients will help you get the boost you need to accomplish your goals. Your capacity to consume those nutrients reduces when you get older, raising your chance of malnutrition. Adult women over 50, for example, are often deficient in vitamin B12 and folate, two nutrients needed for energy production, according to research. B vitamin deficiencies, such as B12 deficiency, can influence your mood, discourage you from losing weight and cause fatigue. As a result, those above the age of 50 can take a high-quality B-complex vitamin to better reduce the risk of deficiency.

17. Limit added sugars.

For weight loss at any age, restricting foods rich in added sugar, such as sweetened drinks, candy, desserts, biscuits, ice cream, sweetened yogurts, and sugary cereals, is important. Since sugar is added to too many ingredients, even things you wouldn't believe, like salad dressing, tomato sauce, and bread, checking the product labeling is the only way to find out whether something has sugar added to it. Check for the terms "added sugars" on the nutrition facts label, or search for traditional sweeteners like high-fructose corn syrup, cane sugar, and agave in the ingredient list.

18. Improve your sleep quality.

Your weight loss efforts can be affected if you do not get sufficiently good sleep. Sleep deficiency has been related to an elevated risk of obesity and has been shown to disrupt weight loss efforts in several reports. A two-year survey of 245 women found that those who slept 7 hours or more a night were 33% more likely to lose weight than those who slept less than 7 hours a night. Weight loss progress is also related to improved sleep efficiency. Reduce the amount of light in your bedroom and stop using your cell or watching TV before bed to get the required 7–9 hours of sleep a night and boost your sleep quality.

19. Be more mindful.

Mindful eating is a simple way to strengthen your interaction with food while still helping you lose weight. Mindful nutrition entails paying closer attention to what you consume and how you eat. It helps you consider your appetite and fullness cues and how food affects your attitude and overall well-being. Many researchers have shown that practicing mindful eating techniques helps people lose weight and change their eating habits. There are no hard and quick guidelines for mindful eating, but eating gently, paying attention to each bite's taste and aroma, and keeping note of how you feel through meals are all simple ways to start mindful eating.

4.2 Beginner Exercise Programs For 50-Year-Old Women

It is never too late to start a workout regimen, whether you are 50, 65, or 80 years old. If you are new to physical exercise, though, it is a smart idea to search for a program designed specifically for beginners. Beginner fitness classes are often slower-paced and have low-impact exercises, lowering the likelihood of injuries. When browsing for a beginner's fitness routine, aim for one that includes a range of workouts, such as yoga, strength training, and aerobic activities. You will be able to practice a range of exercises to get the best out of your class this way.

Several fitness programs for women over 50 are primarily designed to assist in the growth of strength and muscle mass in this age category. Here are some of the programs listed below:

- **Muscles in motion**: Set the music from the 1950s and 1960s, Muscles in Motion, makes you tighten and tone the lower and upper body, emphasizing the abdominal muscles. Resistance bands, hand weights, and exercise balls are used in the group class to gain stamina.

- **S.O.S**: This is the exercise class for you if you are worried about the possibility of osteoporosis or bone damage. It promotes resistance workouts that improve muscle mass and bone health.
- **Popular Silver Sneakers®:** Silver Sneakers workout programs are available free of cost for people on Medicare. Strength training and cardiovascular exercises are emphasized in the traditional program. Modifications are available for those who need extra help or assistance, and the program is tailored for people at all activity levels.

4.3 How Much Exercise Should You Get?

Try to aim for at least 150 minutes of moderate activity or 75 minutes of vigorous activity each week.

How much physical exercise do you get per week? The amount of exercise that is suggested for women over 50 is the same as for other adults. Per week, try to fit in at least 150 minutes of mild or 75 minutes of intense exercise. This equates to 30 minutes of moderate exercise or 15 minutes of intense exercise 5 days a week.

You should split up the workouts into short periods of time, but physicians propose that you should perform physical activity for at least 10 minutes at a time. Strengthening exercises should be done at least twice a week in addition to 150 or 75 minutes of activity.

It is also a smart idea to do balancing workouts at least three times a week if you have reduced mobility and are at risk of falling.

Before beginning a new workout regimen, one thing to keep in mind, particularly if you are new to working out, is that you get your doctor's permission before beginning any new exercise. They will also inform you of the right workouts for women above 50 and the right exercises for you, depending on the health concerns and issues.

Get out and explore while you exercise:

While attending a fitness class or working out at the local YMCA can be a great way to stay in shape while still socializing, keep in mind that you can still do your workouts outdoors. After dinner, heading out for a walk in your neighborhood can be a perfect way of seeing what is going on, getting some fresh air, and keeping the muscles healthy.

You may also take this a step further by heading for a weekend hike, which will encourage you to experience nature while also improving your stamina. Take it easy when you are first learning how to hike. Begin with short hiking on reasonably flat land. If you develop strength and confidence, you can raise the length and intensity of your hikes.

Let us take a closer look at some of the various kinds of workouts that can help you feel better as well as some health effects of fitness for women over 50:

4.4 Best Workouts For Women Over 50

Since not all workouts are created equal, it is important to incorporate a variety of them into your fitness routine. The following are the major types of exercise that are beneficial:

- **Aerobic or cardiovascular:** Aerobic or cardiovascular workouts are also known as endurance exercises, and they must be performed for at least 10 minutes. While the breathing and pulse rate can improve through physical exercise, you can also communicate with a workout partner. Aerobic fitness includes activities such as jogging, walking, and swimming.

- **Stretching**: Stretching movements aim to enhance or retain flexibility, which decreases the likelihood of muscle or joint injury. Yoga is a well-known stretching practice.

- **Balance**: The chance of falling rises as you grow older. Falls may be reduced by doing exercises that help you develop or maintain your equilibrium. Standing on one foot may be a basic balancing workout.

Although there are many different types of exercise, it is important to remember that exercise does not happen in a void. When you exercise, for example, you are improving your cardiovascular system and strengthening your leg muscles. Any strength conditioning exercises may also be used to stretch muscles and improve balance.

- **Strength training:** Lifting weights and workouts involving resistance, such as Pilates or resistance band workouts, are good weight training practices for women over 50. Strength and resistance training is especially important for women over 50 because it can help slow bone loss and reverse muscle loss.

3 Strength training exercises you can try at home:

Although attending a workout class at the local YMCA is a great opportunity to get out and socialize, strength training workouts may also be done from the convenience of your own home. Many of these exercises do not necessarily require the purchase of expensive machinery. You could be good to go as long as you have a couple of hand weights and chairs. A mat will help make it more convenient, but a carpeted floor will work as well.

1. Plank Pose

Planks can also help straighten your posture, which is a plus if you sit in a desk chair for much of the day.

The plank will help you not only enhance and tone your core muscles (abdominal and lower back muscles), but it can also help you improve your equilibrium. Planks will also help you straighten your back, which benefits you if you spend much of your day seated in a desk chair. A plank could be done in a variety of ways. To do a high plank, get into a stance where your arms and legs are upright as if you were at the top of a push-up. A low plank is another choice, which is simpler to do if you are a beginner. Instead of leaning on your hands, bend the arms at the elbows and lean on your forearms to sustain your weight. Keep your back perfectly straight and your head up, regardless of the version you choose. Form a straight line parallel to the floor with the whole body.

2. Squats with a Chair

Squats with a chair are another weight-bearing workout that can be done at home. Squat over a chair as if preparing to sit down, but do not contact the seat during this workout. Instead, you get back up and perform the procedure as many times as necessary. Squats will help you strengthen your balance as well as tone the lower body. When you first begin, you will notice that doing the workout with both hands and arms out in front of you is the most comfortable.

3. Chest Fly

Women's chest muscles are usually weak and underdeveloped. The chest fly is a bodybuilding exercise that makes certain muscles get stronger. You will need a couple of hand weights for this workout. Lie flat on your back on the floor, or on a mat, with your knees bent and feet flat on the ground. Raise your arms over the chest with one weight in each hand. Slowly spread the arms out to the side, lowering the arms and wrists toward the ground while not touching it. Maintain a small bend in the elbows to prevent locking out the arms. Repeat with the arms raised again.

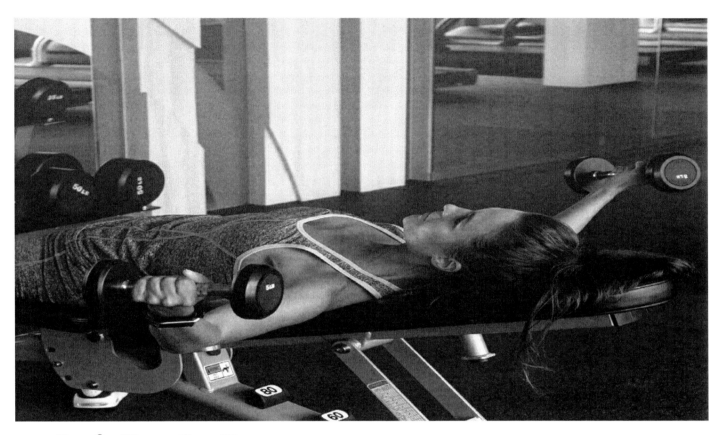

- **Yoga for Women Over 50**

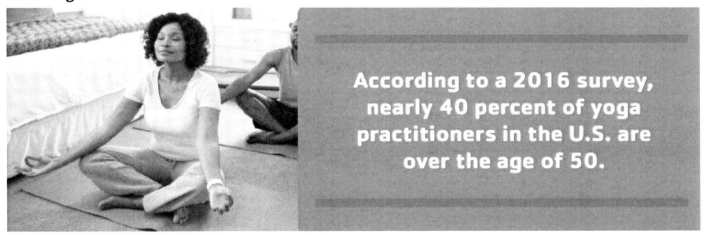

According to a 2016 survey, nearly 40 percent of yoga practitioners in the U.S. are over the age of 50.

Nearly 40% of yoga participants across the United States are over 50, as per a 2016 survey. Some people over 50 have been doing yoga for years or decades, and others are just getting started.

One thing to keep in mind about yoga is that there are various forms to choose from. Regardless of age, some types of yoga can be strenuous, too fast-paced, or physically exhausting for some individuals, while others are intended to be relaxing and gentle. If you are a professional yogi, it is better to stick to the gentler types of yoga, emphasizing balance and stretching over muscle growth and strength.

Chair yoga is one of the easiest ways to get involved in yoga and start a fitness regimen if you have not been physically active in the past. Many of the asanas or poses in chair yoga are performed either sitting or using a seat for support while standing. Chair yoga courses are also available online.

- **Swimming for Women Over 50**

Swimming is an ideal activity for women above the age of 50. Swimming is a low-impact workout, unlike other workouts like walking and running, which can strain the joints. The water surrounds you, serving as a support and cushion, relieving pressure on your joints.

However, do not be misled by its gentleness. Swimming is a great way to have total-body exercise. It will improve your stamina, while also developing your lower and upper body muscles, as well as your heart. Swimming will also help improve the balance by strengthening your core, lowering your chance of falling as you return to land.

4.5 Benefits Of Exercise For Women Over 50

Age is nothing more than a figure. You may be 55, but you appear to be 40 and may sound 35. Alternatively, you may be 50 but appear and sound 65. It all comes down to how much you take care of your body and how you remain active. Many people feel that if they were not active in their twenties, thirties, or forties, there is no sense in starting in their fifties or even later. Fortunately, this is not the case. It is never too late to start a workout regimen. Starting an exercise regimen will help you reverse some of the harmful consequences of inactivity while still helping you feel better about yourself.

The phrase "use 'em or lose 'em" is especially accurate when it comes to your muscles. The typical human loses around 1% of muscle a year, beginning at the age of 50. You do not have to accept muscle failure, however. Even if you are in your 90s, exercise will help you regain muscle mass. The advantages of exercise extend beyond increased muscle mass and stamina. It will also help you maintain good bone health. The body works hard to develop and build bone before you reach the age of around 30. Following that, it is more probable that you will lose bone than gain it. Because of the decrease in hormone intake, bone loss increases even more during menopause.

This is when osteoporosis becomes a significant threat. However, osteoporosis and bone loss are not unavoidable. Weight-bearing workouts, which enable you to work against gravity, will boost your bone density and reduce the likelihood of bone fracture.

Let us look at some of the effects of exercise to relieve common menopause symptoms while we are on the topic of menopause. Weight gain and the growth of excess abdominal fat may occur due to the changes that occur in a woman's body during menopause, such as a decrease in hormone levels. Getting or being active during menopause will help you prevent any weight gain that comes with it. Maintaining a healthy weight will help you prevent diseases like Type 2 diabetes, cancer, and heart failure, linked to being obese or overweight.

4.6 30 days Meal Plan of IF For Women Over 50

These suggested menus contain about 800 calories per day. Don't get too caught up with the number of calories you consume because the amount you ingest differs from person to person and is dependent on the type of food you consume. Pick and choose from the plans; feel free to change your meals and eat your main meal for lunch and vice versa.

1. Week 1 Meal Plan (3 meals per day)

Day 1

Breakfast: Easy Ham & Egg Muffins

Lunch: In a Hurry: Hummus

Dinner: Curry with Coconut Shrimp and Lentils for Dinner

Day 2

Breakfast: Scramble Eggs with Avocado

Lunch: Purple Slaw and Sliced Ham

Dinner: Coconut Broccoli Rice and Prawn Masala

Day 3

Breakfast: Delicious Green Smoothie

Lunch: Chicken and Spinach on Dark Rye Bread

Dinner: Pecorino Mushroom Steak

Day 4

Breakfast: Porridge and Cashew & Chia Seeds

Lunch: Sardines with Yellow and Green Peppers Roasted

Dinner: Veggie Mutton Curry

Day 5

Breakfast: Poached Eggs and Spiced Asparagus Spears

Lunch: Soup with Turmeric and Root Vegetables

Dinner: Chorizo-Spiced Spanish Aubergine Stew

Day 6

Breakfast: Turmeric Spiced Vegetable Casserole

Lunch: Pea & Spinach Soup

Dinner: Low-carb peppered turkey stir-fry

Day 7

Breakfast: Baked Cod and Eggs with Thyme

Lunch: Mushroom-and-Greens Miso Soup

Dinner: Sausage and Mushrooms with Spring Greens

2. Week 2 Meal Plan (3 meals per day)

Day 8

Breakfast: Seasoned Mango Smoothie

Lunch: Noodles with Steamed Pork with Mange Tout Stir-fry

Dinner: Steamed Haddock with Thai Seasonings

Day 9

Breakfast: Pistachio and Chia Seed with Porridge

Lunch: Tapenade & Feta

Dinner: Stir-fried quick Chinese tilapia

Day 10

Breakfast: Boiled Eggs with Seasoned Asparagus

Lunch: Soup with red lentils and almonds

Dinner: Coconut Cauli Rice with Prawn Jalfrezi

Day 11

Breakfast: Mushroom Omelette with Turmeric Spice

Lunch: Salad Jar with Pasta and Pesto

Dinner: Tapenade with Mozzarella

Day 12

Breakfast: Grilled Halibut and Eggs with Basil

Lunch: Crispy Zucchini Canapés

Dinner: Garlicky Shrimp with Mixed Courgetti & Pasta

Day 13

Breakfast: Tomatoes and Herb Omelette

Lunch: Roasted Kale with Coleslaw and Walnuts

Dinner: Salad with Mackerel, Beets, and Red Onions

Day 14

Breakfast: Hashbrowns with Avocado

Lunch: Carrots and Cashews with Miso Aubergine 'Steaks'

Dinner: Lime and Rosemary Chicken Kebabs

3. Week 3 Meal Plan (2 meals per day)

Day 15

Breakfast: Smashed Avocado on Dark Rye Bread

Lunch: -

Dinner: Sausage & Potatoes with Spring Greens

Day 16

Breakfast: -

Lunch: Jalapeno Lime Salmon with Beans & cubed Mango on
Dinner: Prawn Korma with Coconut Cauli Rice

Day 17

Breakfast: Grilled Mackerel and Eggs with Chives

Lunch: -

Dinner: Low-Carb Stir-Fried Peppered Chicken

Day 18

Breakfast: -

Lunch: Lentils Pomegranate and Ricotta Salad

Dinner: Garlicky White Bean Mash with Balsamic Roasted Pork Fillet

Day 19

Breakfast: 2 eggs scrambled with avocado and 1 banana with cranberries

Lunch: -

Dinner: Spanish Courgette Stew with Sausage

Day 20

Breakfast: -

Lunch: Mackerel Salad with Beets and Red Onions

Dinner: Peppered Roast Cod with Nutty Broccoli

Day 21

Breakfast: Muesli with nuts and chia seeds

Lunch: -

Dinner: Turmeric Grilled Cauliflower with Miso

4.   Week 4 Meal Plan (2 meals per day)

Day 22

Breakfast: -

Lunch: Pearl Rice and Pumpkin Seed Salad

Dinner: Peppered Roast Snapper with Nutty Broccoli

Day 23

Breakfast: Pistachio and Chia Seed Porridge

Lunch: -

Dinner: Quick Chinese Mackerel Stir-Fry

Day 24

Breakfast –

Lunch: Lentil Soup with Pesto Sauce

Dinner: Prawn Korma with Coconut Cauli Rice

Day 25

Breakfast: Roasted Halibut and Beans with Chives

Lunch: –

Dinner: Low-Carb Peppered Stir-Fried

Day 26

Breakfast: –

Lunch: Salad with Minted Avocado & Chickpeas

Dinner: Sausage and Potatoes with Baby Spinach

Day 27

Breakfast: Pistachio and Chia Seed Porridge

Lunch: -

Dinner: Bacon Coconut and Veggie Curry

Day 28

Breakfast: –

Lunch: Red Lentil & Coconut Soup with Instant Bacon and Egg Pancakes

Dinner: Noodles with Steamed Pork and fried Mange Tout

Day 29

Breakfast: Muesli with nuts and chia seeds

Lunch: -

Dinner: Turmeric Grilled Cauliflower with Miso

Day 30

Breakfast: -

Lunch: Mackerel Salad with Beets and Red Onions

Dinner: Peppered Roast Cod with Nutty Broccoli

CHAPTER 5: BREAKFAST RECIPES FOR INTERMITTENT FASTING

Breakfast does not have to be difficult. These fast and easy breakfast recipes are easy to make and enjoy on an intermittent fasting diet with only a few ingredients. Here are some delicious and healthy breakfast recipes to start your day.

5.1 Poached eggs and avocado toast

PREP TIME: 15 Minutes

COOK TIME: No

SERVES:2 serving

DIFFICULTY LEVEL: Easy

INGREDIENTS:

- 2 ripe avocados
- 4 eggs
- 2 thick slices of bread
- Juice of a lime or 4tbsp lemon juice
- 1 cup grated Edam cheese
- 1 tbsp freshly ground black pepper
- 2 tbsp salt

- 2 tbsp of butter to spread on the toast

DIRECTIONS:

- Use your general style to poach eggs.
- Meanwhile, take out the stones from the avocados and slice them in half.
  1. Scoop the flesh into a dish or a bowl with a spoon, then add the lime or lemon juice, salt, and pepper.
  2. Using a fork, mash the avocados roughly.
  3. Toast some pieces of bread and spread butter on them.
  4. Cover each slice of the buttered toast with the avocado mixture and a poached egg.
  5. Serve immediately with a sprinkle of grated cheese.
  6. You can serve fresh or fried tomato halves on each side.

5.2 Avocado quesadillas

PREP TIME:30 Minutes

COOK TIME: 10 minutes

SERVES:2 serving

DIFFICULTY LEVEL: Easy

INGREDIENTS:

- 1 peeled and pitted ripe avocado, chop into ¼ inch pieces
- 2 seeded ripe tomatoes, chop into ¼ inch pieces
- 1 tbsp of chopped red onion
- ¼ teaspoon of Tabasco sauce
- 2 tbsp of fresh lemon juice
- 1 tbsp of salt and pepper

- 3 tbsp of chopped fresh coriander
- ¼ cup of sour cream
- ½ teaspoon of vegetable or olive oil
- 24 inches of flour tortillas
- 1 cup shredded Monterey jack cheese

DIRECTIONS:

1. Mix the avocado, lemon juice, tomatoes, onion, and Tabasco in a small bowl.
2. Season with pepper and salt to taste.
3. Mix coriander, sour cream, salt, and pepper to taste in a separate small dish.
4. Brush the tops of the tortillas with oil and place them on a baking sheet.
5. 2 to 4 inches from the heat, broil tortillas until lightly golden.
6. Sprinkle cheese equally over tortillas and broil until melted.
7. To make 2 quesadillas, spread the avocado mixture thinly over 2 tortillas and cover it with 1 of the remaining tortillas with the cheese side down.
8. Slice the quesadillas into four wedges on a cutting board.
9. Serve warm with a spoonful of the sour cream mixture on top of each wedge.

5.3 Mum's supper club tilapia parmesan

PREP TIME: 35 Minutes

COOK TIME: 20 Minutes

SERVES: 1 serving

DIFFICULTY LEVEL: Easy

INGREDIENTS:

- 2 lbs. of tilapia fillets, red or cod snapper could be a substitute
- ½ cup of grated parmesan cheese

- 3 tbsp of mayonnaise
- ¼ teaspoon of salt seasoning
- 3 tbsp of finely chopped green onions
- 2 tbsp of lemon juice
- 4 tbsp of butter kept at room temperature
- ¼ teaspoon of dried basil
- 1 tbsp of dash hot pepper sauce

DIRECTIONS:

1. Preheat the oven to about 350 degrees Fahrenheit.
2. Arrange the fillets in a single layer in a buttered 13-by-9-inch jellyroll pan or a baking dish
3. Do not stack the fillets.
4. Apply some lemon juice on the top.
5. Mix the butter, cheese, onions, mayonnaise, and seasonings in a bowl.
6. With the help of a fork, thoroughly mix all the ingredients.
7. Bake the fish for about 10 to 20 minutes in a preheated oven or until it begins to flake.
8. Spread the cheese mixture on top and bake for 5 minutes or until golden brown.
9. The length of time it takes to bake the fish can be determined by its thickness.
10. Keep an eye on the fish to make sure it does not overcook.

Note: You can also cook the fish in the broiler.

- Broil it for about 3 to 4 minutes or before it is nearly done.
- Add the cheese and Broil for another 2 or 3 minutes, just until the cheese is browned.

5.4 Avocado salad with shrimp/prawn and Cajun potato

PREP TIME: 30 Minutes

COOK TIME: 5 minutes

SERVES:2 serving

DIFFICULTY LEVEL: Easy

INGREDIENTS:

- 1 tbsp of olive oil
- 300g of fresh potatoes
- Some salt to boil potatoes
- 250g or 8oz cooked and peeled king prawns
- 2 freshly sliced spring onions
- 1 minced garlic clove
- 1 peeled, stoned, and diced avocado
- 2 teaspoons of Cajun seasoning
- 1 cup of alfalfa sprout

DIRECTIONS:

1. Cook the potatoes for about 10 to 15 minutes, or until tender, in a medium skillet of lightly salted boiling water. Drain them well.
2. In a large nonstick frying pan, skillet, or a wok, heat the oil.
3. Now add the garlic, prawns, the Cajun seasoning, and spring onions, and fry for about 2-3 minutes until the prawns become hot.
4. Now add the potatoes and cook for another minute.
5. Transfer to the serving dishes and top with some avocado and alfalfa sprouts before serving.

5.5 Black bean burrito and sweet potato

PREP TIME: 1hr and 5mins

SERVES: 8 to 12

PREP TIME: 1 hour 5 Minutes

COOK TIME: 10 Minutes

SERVES:8 serving

DIFFICULTY LEVEL: Easy

INGREDIENTS:

- ½ teaspoon of salt
- 5 cups of peeled and cubed sweet potatoes
- 3 ½ cup of chopped onions
- ½ cup lightly packed cilantro leaf
- 2 teaspoons of vegetable oil or broth
- 1 tbsp of fresh minced green chili pepper
- 4 minced garlic cloves
- 4 teaspoons of ground cumin
- 4 ½ cups of canned black beans
- 4 teaspoons of ground coriander
- 2 tbsp of fresh lemon juice
- 12 flour tortillas (10 inches)
- 1 teaspoon of salt
- Fresh salsa

DIRECTIONS:

1. Preheat the oven to about 350 degrees Fahrenheit.
2. In a medium saucepan, mix the sweet potatoes, salt, and enough water to cover them.
3. Cover it and bring it to a boil, then reduce to low heat and cook until the vegetables are tender for around 10 minutes.
4. Drain the water and put them aside.
5. Heat the oil in a medium saucepan or skillet and add the garlic, onions, and chile while the sweet potatoes are cooking.
6. Cover and cook them on medium-low heat, constantly stirring, for around 7 minutes, or until the onions are soft.
7. Cook while constantly stirring for another 2 to 3 minutes after adding the coriander and cumin.
8. Take the skillet off the heat and put it aside.
9. Mix the cilantro, salt, black beans, lemon juice, and cooked sweet potatoes in a food processor and make puree until smooth (or mash all the ingredients in a large bowl by your hand).
10. Add the spices and cooked onions to the sweet potato mixture in a big mixing bowl.

11. Fill each tortilla with around 2/3 to ¾ cup of the filling, roll it up, and place it seam side down in the baking dish.

12. Bake for 30 minutes, or until smoking hot while tightly covered with foil.

13. Serve with some salsa on top.

5.6 Oatmeal With Pecans & Coconut

PREP TIME: 10 Minutes

COOK TIME: 5 minutes

SERVES:1 serving

DIFFICULTY LEVEL: Easy

INGREDIENTS:

- ½ cup almond or coconut milk
- ½ cup almond or coconut milk
- Chia seeds, 2 tbsp.
- Almond flour (2 tablespoons)
- 1 teaspoon flaxseed meal
- Hemp hearts, 2 tablespoons
- ¼ teaspoon cinnamon powder
- ¼ teaspoon vanilla extract (pure)
- 1 tablespoon toasted and chopped pecans
- 1 tablespoon flakes of coconut

DIRECTIONS

1. Mix the hemp hearts, cinnamon, almond flour, chia seeds, flax meal, milk, and vanilla in a small saucepan.

2. Cook, frequently stirring, until the sauce has thickened, about 5 minutes.

3. Serve immediately after spooning into a bowl and topping with pecans and coconut flakes.

Nutrients Values: Protein 13.4g -Fat 25g- Carbs 7g- Fiber 5g -Net carbs 2g -Calories 312g

5.7 Eggs & Bacon with Cheese Muffins

PREP TIME: 15 Minutes

COOK TIME: 30 minutes

SERVES: 6 serving

DIFFICULTY LEVEL: Moderate

INGREDIENTS

- 6 bacon slices
- 8 large eggs
- A quarter-cup of heavy cream

- Fine sea salt and freshly ground black pepper to taste
- 3 oz. cheddar cheese, shredded

DIRECTIONS

1. Set the oven to 375 degrees Fahrenheit.
2. Grease the bottom and sides of a 6-cup muffin pan generously (Lightly melted butter works great for this).
3. In a cold 12-inch pan, put the bacon and cook it over moderate flame.
4. Cook, flipping once, till crisp all over.
5. Transfer to a plate lined with paper towels.
6. Chop up the bacon into small pieces.
7. Beat everything together like cream, eggs, salt, & pepper in a large mixing dish.
8. Fill every cup of the prepped pan with an equal quantity of cheese and bacon.
9. Over the filling, pour an equal amount of the egg mixture.
10. Bake for 25 to 30 minutes, or until the eggs have puffed up and turned a light golden color.

Nutrients Values: Protein 15g - Carbs 1.5g - Fiber 0g - Fat 26g -Net carbs 1.5g - Calories 303

5.8 Baked Avocado & Eggs With Cheddar Chives

PREP TIME: 10 Minutes

COOK TIME: 15 minutes

SERVES:2 servings

Difficulty Level: Easy

INGREDIENTS

- 2 eggs
- 2 oz. shredded cheddar cheese
- 2 tsp. cream (Heavy)
- 1 teaspoon chives, finely chopped
- Sea salt and freshly ground black pepper
- 1 avocado, pitted and sliced in half

DIRECTIONS

1. Set the oven to 425 degrees Fahrenheit.
2. In a medium mixing bowl, whisk the egg, cheddar, cream, half of the chives, pepper, and salt.
3. Mix everything with a spoon until everything is fully combined.
4. Place the avocados cut side up in a medium-rimmed baking tray (they should fit, so they don't roll around).
5. In the center of each avocado, pour the egg filling.
6. Bake for 12 minutes or until the top of the filling is gently brown.

7. Serve immediately, garnished with the leftover chives.

Nutrients Values: Protein 13g - Carbs 1.3g - Fat 22g - Fiber 0g - Net carbs 1.3g - Calories 257

5.9. Pancakes With Blueberry & Almond

PREP TIME: 10 Minutes

COOK TIME: 5 minutes

SERVES: 10 servings

DIFFICULTY LEVEL: Moderate

INGREDIENTS:

- A quarter-pound of butter
- 2 eggs, big
- A quarter cup of almond milk
- ¼ teaspoon vanilla extract (pure)
- 1 tablespoon flax meal
- ¾ cup almond flour
- 1 teaspoon powdered baking soda
- 1 stevia powder packet
- ¼ teaspoon allspice
- ¼ teaspoon sea salt (optional)
- A third of a cup of blueberries, frozen or fresh, to make the pancakes

DIRECTIONS

1. Whisk together the butter, egg, almond milk, & vanilla in a small mixing dish.
2. In a large mixing bowl, whisk the flour, flax meal, baking powder, stevia, salt, & allspice till thoroughly combined.
3. Add the blueberries and stir to combine.
4. Over moderate flame, heat a nonstick skillet.
5. If the few drops of water swirl over the surface, it's ready to use.
6. In a small saucepan, melt a dollop of butter.
7. Spread a scant ¼ cupful of batter into thin circles in the pan (they'll bubble up).
8. Cook, covered, for 1 to 2 minutes, or until air bubbles emerge on top and the batter seems a bit dry.
9. Cook for another 2 minutes, or till cooked through and brown below.
10. Serve immediately.

Nutrients Values: Protein 3.9g - Carbs 3.9g - Fat 10g - Fiber 1.4g Net carbs 2.5g - Calories 114

5.10 Pork Sausages & Almond Milk

PREP TIME: 10 Minutes

COOK TIME: 45 minutes

SERVES:2 servings

DIFFICULTY LEVEL: Moderate

INGREDIENTS:

- Pork sausages 4 (spicy or sweet)
- 1/3 cup blanched almond flour, fine
- 6 tbsp almond milk
- 3 tablespoons starch
- A quarter-cup of heavy cream
- ¼ teaspoon salt
- 1 egg

DIRECTIONS

1. Preheat the oven to 400°F and set an 8-inch cast-iron pan on the middle rack.
2. In a pan, brown the sausages.
3. Cook for 12 to 15 minutes, flipping once until well browned.
4. Mix the almond flour, starch, almond milk, cream, egg, and salt in a medium mixing bowl.
5. Whisk until everything is properly combined.
6. Put the mixture into the heated pan once the sausages have been browned.
7. Transfer the pan to the oven and bake for 20 to 25 minutes or puffed up and brown.
8. Serve immediately.

Nutrients Values: Protein 16.3g - Carbs 16.2g - Fat 28g - Fiber 2.4g Net carbs 13.8g - Calories 376

5.11 Breakfast Shake With Berries

PREP TIME: 10 Minutes

COOK TIME: No

SERVES:1 serving

DIFFICULTY LEVEL: Easy

INGREDIENTS:

- ¼ cup frozen mixed berries
- ½ cup heavy cream
- ½ cup almond or coconut milk
- 1 tablespoon almond butter
- ½ teaspoon lemon juice, freshly squeezed MCT oil (one tablespoon)

DIRECTIONS

1. In a blender bowl, combine all of the ingredients.
2. Blend until completely smooth.
3. Serve immediately.

NUTRIENTS VALUES: PROTEIN 10G - CARBS 18G - FAT 80G - FIBER 5G - NET CARBS 13G - CALORIES 900

5.12 Omelet With Cheddar Spinach & Mushrooms

PREP TIME: 10 Minutes

COOK TIME: 5 minutes

SERVES:2 servings

DIFFICULTY LEVEL: Moderate

INGREDIENTS:

- 2 tsp olive oil (extra virgin)
- 3 oz. sliced white button mushrooms
- 2 cups baby spinach, packed
- Sea salt
- 6 big eggs, softly beaten
- A handful of fresh parsley, chopped
- 4 oz. shredded cheddar cheese

DIRECTIONS

1. 1 teaspoon oil, heated in the 10inch nonstick pan over medium flame until shimmering Toss in the mushrooms.
2. Cook for 3 to 4 minutes, stirring the skillet several times until the mushrooms are brown.
3. Season with salt and pepper after adding the spinach.
4. Cook for 1 to 2 minutes, or until the spinach is slightly wilted. Place the veggies in a mixing bowl.
5. Set aside after adding the parsley.
6. In the same skillet, heat the remaining teaspoons of oil.
7. Sprinkle the eggs with salt and pepper before pouring them into the pan
8. Cook until the edges of the eggs are set, without moving them.
9. Lift the sides of the egg with a rubber spatula while tilting the pan to allow any uncooked egg to slip beneath and cook.

10. Half of the eggs should be covered in the veggie mixture. On top, grate the cheese.

11. To make a half-moon, fold the plain egg over the half with the veggies.

12. Cook for a further minute.

13. Serve right away.

Nutrients Values: Fat 38g - Protein 34g- Carbs 5g - Fiber 1g - Net carbs 4g - Calories 500

5.13 Blueberry Nut Oatmeal

PREP TIME: 10 Minutes

COOK TIME: 5 minutes

SERVES: 3 servings

DIFFICULTY LEVEL: Easy

INGREDIENTS:

- 1 cup old-fashioned rolled oats 134 cup water
- 1 cup apple grated
- 2 tbsp currants (omit for diabetic and weight-loss diets)
- 1 tablespoon flax seeds, ground
- 1 cup blueberries (fresh or frozen)
- 6 chopped pecan halves
- 6 chopped walnut halves

DIRECTIONS

1. Bring water to a boil in a pan, then add the oats, apples, currants, & flax seeds.
2. Reduce the heat to low and cook for 5 minutes.
3. Add the blueberries, pecans, and walnuts, and mix well.
4. Before serving, turn off the heat, cover, and set aside for 5 mins.

Nutrients Values: Fat 7g - Protein 12g - Carbs 39g - Fiber 6.7g Calories 224

5.14 Overnight Oatmeal

PREP TIME: 10 Minutes (Plus overnight time)

COOK TIME: No

SERVES:3 servings

DIFFICULTY LEVEL: Easy

INGREDIENTS:

- ¼ cup raisins or any dried fruits, diced
- 1 cup rolled oats, old-fashioned
- 2 cups soy, cannabis, or almond milk, unsweetened
- 3 cup freshly crumbled fruits

DIRECTIONS

1. Combine the dried fruit, oats, and non-dairy milk.
2. To soften, cover and chill overnight.
3. Combine fresh diced fruit or defrosted mixed berries in the morning.
4. Enjoy.

Nutrients Values: Fat 5.6g - Protein 12g - Carbs 52g - Fiber 8.1g - Calories 289g

5.15 Fast Banana Berries Breakfast

PREP TIME: 10 Minutes

COOK TIME: 5 minutes

SERVES:2 servings

DIFFICULTY LEVEL: Moderate

INGREDIENTS:

- 2 cups blueberries (fresh or frozen)
- 2 sliced bananas
- ½ cup rolled oats, old-fashioned
- a third of a cup of pomegranate juice
- 1–2 tablespoons walnuts, chopped
- 1 tablespoon sunflower seeds, uncooked
- 2 tbsp. currants (dry)

DIRECTIONS

1. In a small microwave-safe bowl, combine all of the ingredients.
2. Cook for 3 minutes.
3. Enjoy hot.

Nutrients Values: Fat7.5g - Protein 6g; Carbs 74g - Fiber 10.6g - Calories362

5.16 Quinoa Breakfast Pudding

PREP TIME: 10 Minutes

COOK TIME: 5 minutes

SERVES:4 servings

DIFFICULTY LEVEL: Easy

INGREDIENTS:

- A third of a cup of quinoa
- 3 quarts liquid
- 5 Medjool dates or 10 common dates (Deglet Noor), pitting
- 2 cups soy, cannabis, or almond milk, unsweetened
- 1 teaspoon vanilla extract
- A quarter-cup of sliced almonds
- 1/8 cup walnuts, roughly ground
- ½ cup raisins, dry
- 1 cup baby spinach, coarsely chopped
- 1 cup kale leaves, finely chopped
- A quarter teaspoon of cinnamon

DIRECTIONS

1. Prep the oven to 350 degrees Fahrenheit.
2. Quinoa should be rinsed and drained using a fine mesh sieve.
3. Bring 3 cups of water and quinoa to a boil in a medium skillet.
4. Reduce heat to low and cook, uncovered, for approximately 20 minutes, or until the grains are transparent and the mixture has the consistency of thick porridge.
5. Grind soy milk, dates, and vanilla in a blender.
6. Toss the cooked quinoa with this mixture.
7. Combine the spinach, currants, kale, and nuts in a mixing bowl. Sprinkle cinnamon over the top and bake for 30 minutes in a lightly greased 9-inch square baking pan.
8. Serve hot or chilled.

Nutrients Values: Fat8.5g - Protein 13g - Carbs 60 - Fiber 7.5g -Calories 347

5.17 Berries With Butternut Breakfast

PREP TIME: 10 Minutes

COOK TIME: 15 minutes

SERVES:4 servings

DIFFICULTY LEVEL: Easy

INGREDIENTS:

- 1 small butternut squash, deseeded, peeled, and cut into ½ -inch pieces (approx. 1 pound)
- 2 peeled, cut into chunks, and cored, medium apples with a pinch of cinnamon
- Nutmeg (1 teaspoon)
- ¾ cup of water
- 2 cups wild blueberries, frozen
- ½ cup walnuts, chopped
- ½ cup currants or raisins

DIRECTIONS

1. In a saucepan, combine the nutmeg, apples, squash, cinnamon, and water.
2. Bring to a boil, turn to low heat, cover, and simmer for 15 minutes, or until tender.
3. If necessary, add additional water.
4. Using a potato masher, mash the ingredients until it is choppy.
5. Mix well to combine the frozen berries, raisins, and walnuts.
6. Spoon the blueberry mixture on top of the mashed butternut squash.

Nutrients Values: Fat 10.5g - Protein 6g - Carbs 49g - `Fiber 8g - Calories 280

5.18 Egg Plant in Slow cooker

PREP TIME: 10 Minutes

COOK TIME: 1 hour

SERVES: 2 servings

DIFFICULTY LEVEL: Easy

INGREDIENTS:

- ½ inch cubes from 1 medium eggplant
- 2 cups tomato, diced
- 1 cup minced onion
- 1 ½ cup cooked garbanzo beans (chickpeas)
- 1 cored and chopped apple
- ½ cup carrot juice
- 1 ½ cup low-sodium or no-salt vegetable broth
- Tomato paste, 6 oz.
- A pinch of cinnamon
- Nutmeg (½ teaspoon)

DIRECTIONS

1. Combine the eggplant, onions, beans, tomato, and apple in a saucepan.
2. Carrot juice, vegetable broth, tomato paste, cinnamon, and nutmeg should all be combined.

3. Pour the sauce over the veggies.

4. Cook for 1 hour on low heat, covered.

5. Enjoy hot.

Nutrients Values: Fat 4.3g - Protein 18g - Carbs 59g - Fiber 12.9g - Calories 310

5.19 Breakfast Butternut Hot Soup

PREP TIME: 15 Minutes

COOK TIME: 30 minutes

SERVES: 6 servings

DIFFICULTY LEVEL: Easy

INGREDIENTS:

- 4 cups butternut squash, frozen
- 2 medium chopped, deseeded, and peeled apples
- 4 cups chopped frozen kale
- 1 cup onion, chopped
- 2 tbsp vinegar with a fruity taste
- 5 cups carrot juice
- ½ cup soy, almond, or cannabis milk, unsweetened
- ½ cup cashews, raw
- A quarter cup of hemp seeds
- A pinch of cinnamon
- Nutmeg (½ teaspoon)

DIRECTIONS

1. Combine the onion, apples, vinegar, squash kale, and carrot juice in a saucepan.

2. Bring to a boil, then reduce to low heat, cover, and continue to cook for 30 minutes, or till the kale becomes very soft.

3. In a blender or high-powered processor, blend half of the broth with the milk, cashews, & hemp seeds.

4. Toss the combined ingredients back into the soup pot.

5. Mix in the cinnamon and nutmeg.

Nutrients Values: Fat 6.6g - Protein 8g – Carbs 49g – Fiber 6.7g - Calories 260

5.20 Divine Apples

PREP TIME: 10 Minutes

COOK TIME: 15 minutes

SERVES: 4 servings

DIFFICULTY LEVEL: Easy

INGREDIENTS:

- 6 cored, peeled, and diced apples, divided
- 2 tsp cinnamon powder
- ½ cup walnuts, chopped
- 3 sliced dates
- 2 tbsp flax seeds (ground)
- ¼ cup soy, almond, or cannabis milk, unsweetened
- ½ cup raisins
- ½ cup oats, old-fashioned

DIRECTIONS

1. Set the oven to 350 degrees Fahrenheit.
2. Mix 1 cup of the diced apples, cinnamon, walnuts, dates, flax seeds, and soy milk in a high-powered blender.
3. Cover the remaining chopped apples with the blended batter in a baking dish. Mix in the raisins well.
4. Oats should be sprinkled on top.
5. Cook for 15 minutes in the oven.
6. Enjoy hot.

Nutrients Values: Fat 11.8g - Protein 10g - Carbs 58g - Fiber 9.1g - Calories 331

5.21 Fruity Breakfast Salad

PREP TIME: 15 Minutes

COOK TIME: No

SERVES: 2 servings

DIFFICULTY LEVEL: Easy

INGREDIENTS:

- 1 Boston lettuce head, split into small pieces
- 1 cup fennel bulb, thinly sliced
- 1 medium peeled cucumber, finely cut in rounds and halved
- ¼ cup chopped walnuts
- 1 peeled and sliced apple
- 2 peeled and cored apples
- ¼ teaspoon cinnamon

DIRECTIONS

1. Toss together fennel, apple, lettuce, cucumber, & walnuts in a salad bowl.
2. In a high-powered processor, puree the remaining apples, orange, and cinnamon until smooth.
3. Toss the salad with the combined dressing.

Nutrients Values: Fat 10.4g - Protein 10g - Carbs 45g - Fiber 9.5g - Calories 273

5.22 Scrambled Tuscan Tofu

PREP TIME: 10 Minutes

COOK TIME: 5 minutes

SERVES: 2 servings

DIFFICULTY LEVEL: Easy

INGREDIENTS:

- 3 scallions (whole) diced
- ½ cup red bell pepper, finely chopped
- 2 garlic cloves, minced or pressed
- 1 large tomato, chopped
- 2 cups shredded firm tofu, drained
- A seasoning mix with no salt that may be adjusted to taste
- 1 tablespoon dietary yeast
- 5 oz. roughly chopped baby spinach
- 1 tsp Bragg Liquid Amino
- To taste freshly ground pepper

DIRECTIONS

1. Saute garlic, red pepper, scallions, and tomato in ¼ cup water in a big pan over medium-high heat for 5 minutes.
2. Cook for a further 5 minutes after adding the other ingredients.
3. Serve.

Nutrients Values: Fat 2.7g - Protein 12g - Carbs 28g - Fiber 5.1g - Calories 164

5.23 Frittata di Polenta

PREP TIME: 10 Minutes

COOK TIME: 5 minutes

SERVES: 6 servings

DIFFICULTY LEVEL: Easy

INGREDIENTS:

- 6 garlic cloves, minced
- 1 bunch kale or collards
- 1 tsp oregano (oregano)
- Italian spice combination with no salt, to taste

- 1 teaspoon mustard powder
- A quarter teaspoon of black pepper
- A third of a spoonful of nutritional yeast
- 1 cup cornmeal, roughly ground (not instant)

DIRECTIONS

1. 2 to 3 minutes over medium heat, water-sauté garlic.
2. Add veggies, oregano, & MatoZest or another no-salt Italian seasoning mix, and simmer for 10 to 15 minutes or until greens are cooked.
3. In a separate dish, bring 4 cups of water to a boil.
4. Add the dry mustard, pepper, and nutritional yeast, then toss in the cornmeal and cook for another 5 minutes while whisking.
5. Reduce to low heat and add the greens.
6. Cook for a further 10 minutes, occasionally stirring (till a wooden spoon can nearly stand up in the pan).
7. Pour into a baking dish that has been lightly greased with olive oil and set aside for three hours to harden up.
8. Before serving, reheat in the oven.

Nutrients Values: Fat 0.6g - Protein 4g- Carbs 23g - Fiber 2.8g - Calories 114

5.24 Berry Parfait

PREP TIME: 20 Minutes (Plus one hour for chill)

COOK TIME: No

SERVES:4 servings

DIFFICULTY LEVEL: Easy

INGREDIENTS:

- 1 cup vanilla rice milk
- ½ cup plain cream cheese
- 1 tbsp sugar (granulated)
- ½ teaspoon cinnamon powder
- 1 cup Meringue Cookies, crumbled
- 2 cups blueberries, fresh
- 1 cup fresh strawberries, sliced

DIRECTIONS

1. Blend all the ingredients like sugar, cream cheese, milk, & cinnamon in a small bowl until smooth.
2. Place ¼ cup of crushed cookie in the bottom of 4 (6-ounce) glasses.
3. Top the cookies with ¼ cup of the cream cheese mixture.
4. ¼ cup of berries should be placed on top of the cream cheese.

5. Repeat with the cookies, cream cheese mixture, and berries in each cup.

6. Refrigerate for one hour before serving.

Nutrients Values: Fat 11g - Carbs 33g - Fiber 84mg - Protein 4g- Calories: 243

5.25 Hot Cereal With Mixed Grains

PREP TIME: 10 Minutes

COOK TIME: 25 minutes

SERVES:4 servings

DIFFICULTY LEVEL: Easy

INGREDIENTS:

- 2 ¼ cups of water
- 1 ¼ cup rice milk (vanilla)
- 6 tbsp bulgur (uncooked)
- 2 tbsp. whole buckwheat, uncooked
- 1 apple, peeled and sliced
- 6 tablespoons couscous, uncooked
- ½ teaspoon cinnamon powder

DIRECTIONS

1. Boil the water & milk in a pot over medium heat.

2. Toss in the bulgur, buckwheat, & apple, and bring to a boil.

3. Lower the heat and cook for 25 to 30 minutes, or till the bulgur is cooked, stirring periodically.

4. Mix in the couscous & cinnamon after removing the pot from the heat.

5. Allow 10 minutes to settle, and covered, before fluffing the cereal with a fork and dishing.

Nutrients Values: Fat 2.3 g – Protein 15g – Carbs 48g – Fiber 11.8 g - Calories 246

5.26 Pudding With Corn

PREP TIME: 10 Minutes

COOK TIME: 40 minutes

SERVES:6 servings

DIFFICULTY LEVEL: Moderate

INGREDIENTS:

- Grease the baking dish with unsalted butter
- 2 tbsp flour (all-purpose)
- ½ tbsp baking soda
- Three eggs
- ¾ cup room temperature unsweetened rice milk

- 3 tablespoons melted unsalted butter
- 2 tablespoons sour cream (mild)
- 2 tbsp. sugar (granulated)
- 2 cups thawed frozen corn kernels

DIRECTIONS

1. Set the oven to 350 degrees Fahrenheit.
2. Set aside an 8-by-8-inch baking dish that has been lightly greased with butter.
3. Combine the flour & baking soda in a small dish and put aside.
4. Whisk together the eggs, rice milk, butter, sour cream, and sugar in a medium mixing dish.
5. In a separate bowl, whisk together the flour, baking powder, and salt until smooth.
6. Stir the corn into the batter until it is thoroughly combined.
7. Bake for about forty minutes, or once the pudding is set, after spooning the mixture into the baking dish.
8. Allow 15 minutes for the pudding to cool before serving warm.

Nutrients Values: Fat: 1g - Protein: 4g - Carbs: 34g- Calories: 159

5.27 Bread Pudding With Rhubarb

PREP TIME: 15 Minutes

COOK TIME: 50 minutes

SERVES: 6 servings

DIFFICULTY LEVEL: Easy

INGREDIENTS:

- ½ cup rice milk, unsweetened
- Three eggs
- ½ cup sugar, granulated
- Cornstarch, 1 tablespoon
- 10 thick slices of white bread, sliced into 1-inch sections
- 1 vanilla bean, split
- 2 cups fresh rhubarb, chopped

DIRECTIONS

1. Set the oven to 350 degrees Fahrenheit.
2. Set aside an 8-by-8-inch baking tray that has been lightly greased with butter.
3. Blend the rice milk, eggs, sugar, and cornstarch in a large mixing dish.
4. Put the vanilla beans into the milk and whisk to mix them. Stir the bread into the egg mixture until it is fully coated.
5. Stir in the rhubarb, which has been diced.

6. Allow 30 minutes for the bread and egg mix to soak.

7. Fill the baking dish half with the mixture, cover with aluminum foil, and bake for forty minutes.

8. Remove the bread pudding from the oven and bake for a further 10 minutes, or till golden brown and done.

9. Warm the dish before serving.

Nutrients Values: Fat 4g - Carbs 35g- Fiber 109mg - Protein 6g - Calories 197

CHAPTER 6: LUNCH RECIPES FOR INTERMITTENT FASTING

Are you looking for lunch ideas? If you are on an intermittent fasting diet plan, consider these meals as they are easy and nutritious lunch recipes for you to try and enjoy.

6.1 Sweet potato curry with chickpeas and spinach

PREP TIME: 30 Minutes

COOK TIME: 15 minutes

SERVES: 6 servings

DIFFICULTY LEVEL: Easy

INGREDIENTS:

- ½ cup thinly sliced sweet onions
- ½ tablespoon canola oil
- 2 teaspoons of curry powder
- 1 tbsp of cumin
- 1 teaspoon of cinnamon

- 10oz washed, stemmed, and coarsely chopped fresh spinach
- 2 large peeled and diced sweet potatoes
- 1 can of rinsed and drained chickpeas
- ½ cup of water
- 1 can of diced tomatoes
- ¼ cup of chopped fresh cilantro for garnishing
- Brown rice or basmati rice for serving

DIRECTIONS:

- You can cook your sweet potatoes in whatever way you like.
- You can peel, slice, and steam them for around 15 minutes in a veggie steamer.
- Baking or boiling are both feasible choices.
- Heat 1-2 tsp vegetable or canola oil over medium heat as sweet potatoes are cooking.
- Now add the onions and cook for 2-3 minutes, or before they soften.
- Add in the cumin, curry powder, and cinnamon and stir to cover the onions in spices properly.
- Mix in the tomatoes and their juices, as well as the chickpeas, and stir to combine.
- Raise the temperature to a strong boil for around a minute or two after adding a half cup of water.
- Then, a few handfuls at a time, add the fresh spinach, stirring to cover with the cooking liquid.
- When all the spinach has been added to the pan, cover it, cook for 3 minutes, or until it is just wilted.
- Now add the cooked sweet potatoes into the liquid and stir them.
- Cook for the next 3-5 minutes, or until all the flavors are well mixed.
- Serve immediately after transferring to a serving dish and toss with some fresh cilantro.
- This recipe goes well with brown or basmati rice as well.

6.2 Grilled lemon salmon

PREP TIME: 30 Minutes

COOK TIME: 15 minutes

SERVES: 4 servings

DIFFICULTY LEVEL: Easy

INGREDIENTS:

- ½ tbsp of pepper
- 2 tbsp of fresh dill
- ½ tbsp of salt
- ½ lbs. salmon fillets
- ½ tbsp garlic powder
- ½ cup packed brown sugar
- 3 tbsp of oil
- 1 chicken bouillon cube mixed with 2 tbsp of water
- 2 tbsp of soy sauce
- 1 thinly sliced lemon
- 4 tbsp of finely chopped green onions
- 2 slices of onions, separated into rings

DIRECTIONS:

1. Season the salmon with dill, salt, pepper, and garlic powder.
2. Place in a small glass pan.

3. Mix the sugar, oil, chicken bouillon, green onions, and soy sauce in a large bowl.
4. Pour the mixture over the salmon and refrigerate for 1 hour, turning once.
5. Drain the marinade and toss it back.
6. Preheat the grill to medium heat and place the lemon and the onion on top.
7. Cover and Cook for 15 minutes, or until the fish is cooked properly.

6.3 The best-baked potatoes

PREP TIME: 1 hour 10 Minutes

COOK TIME: 1 hour

SERVES: 1 serving

DIFFICULTY LEVEL: Easy

INGREDIENTS:

- 1 large russet potato
- 1 tbsp of Kosher Salt
- 2 tbsp canola oil

DIRECTIONS:

- Preheat the oven to 350 degrees Fahrenheit and place racks in the upper and bottom thirds.
- Wash the potato or potatoes vigorously under cool running water with a stiff brush.
- Dry and then poke 8 to 12 deep holes all over the spud with a regular fork to allow moisture to escape while cooking.
- Place in a bowl with a thin coating of oil.

- Season with kosher salt and put directly on the oven's middle rack.
- To collect some drippings, place a baking sheet like aluminum foil on the lower shelf.
- Bake for 1 hour, or until the skin is crisp, but the flesh underneath is tender.
- Serve by forming a dotted line with your fork from end to end, pressing the ends together to crack the spud open. It will easily open. But be alert as there will be steam.

Note: If you are cooking more than four potatoes, you will need to add up to 15 minutes to the cooking period.

6.4 Vegan fried Fish tacos

PREP TIME: 50mins

SERVES: 2

PREP TIME: 50 Minutes

COOK TIME: 15 minutes

SERVES: 2 servings

DIFFICULTY LEVEL: Easy

INGREDIENTS:

- 2 cups of panko breadcrumbs
- 14oz of silken tofu
- ½ teaspoon salt
- ½ cup of plain flour
- 1 teaspoon smoked paprika

- 1 teaspoon ground cumin
- ½ teaspoon cayenne pepper
- ½ cup of non-dairy milk
- ½ head of finely shredded cabbage
- 2 tbsp of vegetable oil for frying
- 8 small tortillas
- 1 ripe avocado
- 2 tbsp vegan mayonnaise to serve

Pickled onion:

- 1 peeled and finely sliced red onion
- 1 tbsp of sugar
- ½ cup of apple cider vinegar
- 1 teaspoon of salt

DIRECTIONS:

1. To absorb extra moisture, pat the tofu with a few sheets of kitchen paper. Cut the tofu into small 1-inch pieces with a knife.
2. In a large shallow bowl, add the breadcrumbs.
3. Mix the flour, smoked paprika, salt, cayenne, and cumin in a separate large shallow bowl.
4. In a third wide shallow bowl, pour the milk.
5. Toss the tofu chunks in the flour, then the milk, then the breadcrumbs, and put them on a baking sheet.
6. Load a large frying pan with vegetable oil to a depth of 1/2 inch. Place over medium heat and allow the oil to heat up. Fry blocks of breaded tofu until golden underneath, then turn and continue frying until golden all over. To drain, put on a baking sheet lined with kitchen paper. Do the same for the remaining tofu.

For the pickled onion:

1. In a small kettle, heat the apple cider vinegar, salt, and some sugar until steaming.
2. Pour the hot vinegar over the thinly sliced red onion into a container or bowl.
3. Enable it to soften and turn pink, so let it sit for at least 30 minutes.
4. Served hot fried tofu with pickled onion, vegan mayo, avocado, and shredded cabbage in warmed tortillas. You can warm them over a lit gas ring on the stove.

6.5 Baked Mahi

PREP TIME: 20 Minutes

COOK TIME: 10 minutes

SERVES: 4 servings

DIFFICULTY LEVEL: Easy

INGREDIENTS:

- Juice of a lemon
- 2 lbs. of Mahi (4 fillets)
- 1 cup breadcrumbs
- 1 teaspoon salt
- 1 cup mayonnaise
- ¼ teaspoon ground black pepper
- ½ cup finely chopped white onion

DIRECTIONS:

1. Preheat the oven to 425 degrees Fahrenheit.
2. Place the fish in a baking dish after rinsing it. Squeeze some lemon juice over the fish, then season with salt and pepper.
3. Spread mayonnaise and sliced onions on the fish. Bake for 25 minutes at 425°F with breadcrumbs on top.

Nutrients Values: Fat 14g - Protein 11g - Carbs 20g –Fiber 6g - Calories 236

6.6 Veggies & Salmon Kedgeree

PREP TIME: 10 Minutes

COOK TIME: 20 minutes

SERVES: 4 servings

DIFFICULTY LEVEL: Easy

INGREDIENTS:

- ½ tsp. curry powder
- 1 pound skinless hot-smoked salmon portions, flaked
- ½ cup vegetable mix
- Sea salt and pepper, to taste
- One green onion, thinly sliced
- 1 cup basmati rice
- 2 tbsp. extra virgin olive oil

DIRECTIONS

1. Add rice to a saucepan of boiling salted water, turn heat to low, and cook for about 12 minutes, covered, until just tender.
2. In a pan set over medium heat, add extra virgin olive oil and cook the onion, stirring until tender, for approximately 3 minutes.
3. Stir in the curry powder and proceed to cook for about 1 minute until fragrant. Stir in the rice until well mixed, then add the salmon, vegetables, salt, and pepper.
4. Keep cooking until fully cooked, around 3 minutes.
5. Just serve.

Nutrients Values: Fat: 25g - Carbs: 34g - Protein: 20g - Calories: 291

6.7 Baked Sardines with Wilted Rocket salad

PREP TIME: 15 Minutes

COOK TIME: 10 minutes

SERVES: 4 servings

DIFFICULTY LEVEL: Easy

INGREDIENTS:

- 2 large bunches of baby arugula, trimmed
- 16 fresh sardines, innards, and gills removed
- 2 tsp. extra virgin olive oil
- Sea salt
- Freshly ground black pepper
- Lemon wedges, for garnish

DIRECTIONS

1. Get your outdoor grill or a stove-top griddle ready.
2. Rinse arugula under running water, shake off excess water, place them on a dish; set them aside.

3. Remove the scales, rinse the sardines in water and rub them; wipe them dry and mix in a large bowl with extra virgin olive oil.
4. Toss it to coat it.
5. Place the sardines over the grill and grill on each side for approximately 3 minutes or until golden brown and crispy.
6. Season with sea salt and pepper and pass directly to the arugula-lined platter.
7. Serve immediately with garnished lemon wedges.

Nutrients Values: Fat: 35g - Carbs: 26g - Protein: 17g - Calories: 289

6.8 Curry Salmon with Black Cabbage

PREP TIME: 15 Minutes

COOK TIME: 45 minutes

SERVES: 4 servings

DIFFICULTY LEVEL: Easy

INGREDIENTS:

- A pinch of coarse salt
- 2 tbsp. extra virgin olive oil
- A pinch of ground black pepper
- 1 cup brown basmati rice
- Lime wedges for serving
- One pound (½ head) of black cabbage, sliced crosswise
- 4 (6 ounces each) salmon fillets
- ¼ cup freshly squeezed lime juice
- ½ cup fresh mint leaves
- 1 pound carrots, coarsely grated
- 2 tsp. curry powder

DIRECTIONS

1. In a large saucepan set over medium-low heat, bring two cups of water to a gentle boil; add rice and season with sea salt and pepper; turn the heat to low and cook, covered, for about 35 minutes.
2. Meanwhile, in a wide bowl, mix black cabbage, extra virgin olive oil, lime juice, mint, carrots, salt, and black pepper; toss until well blended.
3. Put 4 inches of heat on the broiler rack and preheat it.
4. Place the salmon on a foil-lined baking sheet and rub it with curry, salt, and pepper.
5. Broil the fish for about eight minutes or until it is just cooked.
6. With the green Salad and grilled salmon, serve the cooked rice.

Nutrients Values: Fat: 9g - Carbs: 6g - Protein: 1g - Calories: 105

6.9 Pasta & Shrimps

PREP TIME: 15 Minutes

COOK TIME: 5 minutes

SERVES: 4 servings

DIFFICULTY LEVEL: Easy

INGREDIENTS:

- 2 tsp. extra virgin olive oil
- ¼ cup thinly sliced fresh basil
- 2 tbsp. capers, drained
- 3 garlic cloves, crushed
- 1 pound shrimp, peeled, deveined
- 2cups chopped plum tomato
- ⅓ cup pitted olives (chopped)
- 4 cups hot cooked pasta
- ¼ cup feta cheese (crumbled)
- ¼ tsp. black pepper
- Cooking spray

DIRECTIONS

1. Heat extra virgin olive oil in a medium nonstick pan and set over medium flame; add garlic and fry for approx. Thirty-five seconds.
2. Add shrimp and sauté for an additional 1 minute.
3. Stir in the basil & tomatoes and bring to medium-low heat; simmer for 5 minutes or till the tomatoes are soft.
4. Stir in capers, black pepper & olives.
5. Combine the pasta and shrimp mixture in a medium bowl; toss to blend and top with the cheese.
6. Instantly serve.

Nutrients Values: Fat: 7.7g - Protein: 6g - Carbs: 52g - Fiber: 7.3g - Calories: 277

6.10 Grilled Codfish

Total time: 40 minutes

Prep time: 10 minutes

Cook time: 30 minutes

Yields: 4 servings

INGREDIENTS

PREP TIME: 20 Minutes

COOK TIME: 10 minutes

SERVES: 4 servings

DIFFICULTY LEVEL: Easy

INGREDIENTS:

- 1 tbsp. olive oil
- 1 (14-oz) can drain artichoke hearts
- Four cloves of garlic, crushed

- One green bell pepper, cut into small strips
- ½ cup halved pitted olives
- 1-pint cherry tomatoes1 tbsp. fennel seed
- 1 ½ lb. cod, quartered
- 4 ½ tsp. grated orange peel
- 2 tbsp. drained capers⅓ to ½ cup fresh orange juice
- A pinch of ground pepper
- A pinch salt

DIRECTIONS

1. Preheat your oven to 450 ° F. A 10-15-inch baking pan is generously greased with one tablespoon of olive oil.
2. Arrange the artichoke hearts, garlic, bell pepper, olives, tomatoes, and fennel seeds in the prepared pan.
3. Place the Codfish and top with orange peel, capers, orange juice, pepper, and salt over the vegetables.

Nutrients Values: Protein 15g - Carbs 1.5g - Fiber 0g - Fat 26g -Net carbs 1.5g - Calories 303

6.11 Baked Sole

PREP TIME: 20 Minutes

COOK TIME: 50 minutes

SERVES: 4 servings

DIFFICULTY LEVEL: Easy

INGREDIENTS:

- 2 tsp. extra virgin olive oil
- 1 large sliced onion
- 1 tbsp. orange zest
- ¼ cup orange juice
- ¼ cup lemon juice
- ¾ cup apple juice
- 1 minced clove of garlic
- 1 (16 oz.) can of whole tomatoes, drained and coarsely chopped, the juice reserved
- ½ cup reserved tomato juice
- 1 bay leaf
- ½ tsp. crushed dried basil
- ½ tsp. crushed dried thyme
- ½ tsp. crushed dried oregano
- 1 tsp. crushed fennel seeds
- A pinch of black pepper
- 1 lb. fish fillets (perch, Flounder, or sole)

DIRECTIONS

1. In a large nonstick skillet set over medium heat, add oil.
2. For around 5 minutes or until tender, sauté the onion in the oil.

3. Add all the remaining ingredients, except for the fish.
4. Simmer uncovered for 30 minutes or so.
5. Arrange the fish and cover it with the sauce in a baking dish.
6. When tested with a fork, bake the fish at 375°F, uncovered, for about 15 minutes or until it flakes easily.

Nutrients Values: Fat8.5g - Protein 13g - Carbs 60 - Fiber 7.5g -Calories 347

6.12 Spanish Cod

Total time: 35 minutes

Prep time: 20 minutes

Cook time: 15 minutes

Yield: 6 servings

INGREDIENTS

PREP TIME: 20 Minutes

COOK TIME: 15 minutes

SERVES: 6 servings

DIFFICULTY LEVEL: Easy

INGREDIENTS:

- 1 tbsp. extra virgin olive oil
- 1 tbsp. butter¼ cup onion, finely chopped
- 2 tbsp. garlic, chopped
- 1 cup tomato sauce
- 15 cherry tomatoes, halved
- ¼ cup deli marinated Italian vegetable salad, drained and chopped
- ½ cup green olives, chopped
- One dash of cayenne pepper
- One dash of black pepper
- One dash paprika
- Six cod fillets

DIRECTIONS

1. Over medium heat, put a large skillet and add the olive oil and butter.
2. Attach the garlic and onion and cook until the garlic begins to brown.
3. Apply the sauce and tomatoes to the tomatoes and let them simmer.
4. Stir in the vegetables, olives, and spices that have been marinated.
5. Over medium heat, cook the fillet in the sauce for 8 minutes.
6. Instantly serve

Nutrients Values: Protein 3.9g - Carbs 3.9g - Fat 10g - Fiber 1.4g Net carbs 2.5g - Calories 114

6.13 Ancient Salmon Burgers

Total time: 30 minutes

Prep time: 15 minutes

Cook time: 15 minutes

Yield: 4 servings

INGREDIENTS

PREP TIME: 20 Minutes

COOK TIME: 10 minutes

SERVES: 4 servings

DIFFICULTY LEVEL: Easy

INGREDIENTS:

- 1 pound skinless salmon fillets, diced
- 1 large egg white
- ½ cup panko
- 1 pinch of sea salt
- ¼ tsp. freshly ground black pepper
- ½ cup cucumber slices
- ¼ cup crumbled feta cheese
- 4 (2.5-oz) toasted ciabatta rolls

DIRECTIONS

1. In a food processor, combine the salmon, egg white, and panko; pulse until the salmon is finely chopped.
2. Shape four 4-inch patties with the salmon mixture and season with sea salt and pepper.
3. Heat the grill and cook the patties over medium-high heat, rotating once, about 7 minutes per hand, or until just cooked through.
4. Serve with preferred toppings and buns (such as sliced cucumbers and feta).

Nutrients Values: Fat: 1g - Protein: 4g - Carbs: 34g- Calories: 159

6.14 Grilled Tuna

PREP TIME: 10 Minutes (One hour chill time)

COOK TIME: 6 minutes

SERVES: 4 servings

DIFFICULTY LEVEL: Easy

INGREDIENTS:

- 4 tuna steaks,

- 3 tbsp. extra virgin oil
- ½ cup hickory wood chips, soaked
- Sea salt
- Freshly ground black pepper
- Juice of 1 lime

DIRECTIONS

1. Put the Tuna and olive oil in a zip-lock plastic container, seal, and refrigerate for an hour.
2. Have a charcoal or gas grill packed.
3. When using a coal grill, sprinkle a handful of hickory wood chips when the coals are warm for added spice.
4. Grease the grill grate gently.
5. With salt and pepper, season the Tuna and cook on the grill for about 6 minutes, turning just once.
6. Transfer to a dish.
7. Drizzle over the fish with the lime juice and serve immediately.

Nutrients Values: Fat 3.3g - Protein 15g - Carbs 65g -Fiber 10.6g - Calories 335

6.15 Quick Halibut Dish

PREP TIME: 15 Minutes

COOK TIME: 30 minutes

SERVES: 4 servings

DIFFICULTY LEVEL: Easy

INGREDIENTS:

- Four fillets of halibut (6 ounces)
- 1 tbsp. Greek seasoning
- 1 tbsp. lemon juice
- ¼ cup olive oil
- ¼ cup capers
- 1 jar (5 ounces) pitted Kalamata olives
- 1 chopped onion
- 1 large tomato, chopped
- A pinch of freshly ground black pepper
- A pinch of salt

DIRECTIONS

1. Preheat your 250 ° F oven.
2. Arrange the fillets of halibut on a sheet of aluminum foil and sprinkle them with Greek seasoning.
3. Combine the lemon juice, olive oil, capers, olives, onion, tomato, salt, and pepper in a bowl; spoon the mixture over the fillets and fold to seal the foil's edges.
4. Place the folded foil and bake for approximately 40 minutes or until the fish flakes easily when touched with a fork on a baking sheet.

Nutrients Values: Fat7.5g - Protein 6g; Carbs 74g - Fiber 10.6g - Calories362

6.16 Grilled Garlic Lamb Chops

PREP TIME: 20 Minutes

COOK TIME: 30 minutes

SERVES: 4 servings

DIFFICULTY LEVEL: Moderate

INGREDIENTS:

- 8 lamb chops (4–5 ounces)
- 4 fresh garlic cloves, coarsely chopped
- ½ tbsp rosemary (dry)
- If desired, season with garlic salt to taste
- Three teaspoons of oil Mustard dijon
- 1 lemon, squeezed
- 1 teaspoon of honey
- 2 tbsp extra-virgin olive oil
- A quarter teaspoon of red wine vinegar
- To taste freshly ground pepper
- Garnish with fresh mint leaves

DIRECTIONS

1. Preheat the oven to broil.
2. Chops should be rinsed in cold water and dried with paper towels.
3. Place them on a grilling pan in a thin layer and set them aside.
4. In a small mixing dish, mix the garlic and rosemary.
5. Rub the garlic/rosemary mixture onto both sides of the chops, season with garlic salt if preferred, and broil for about 4 inches.
6. Broil until the desired doneness is reached.
7. While the chops are broiling, mix vinegar, lime juice, honey, olive oil, mustard, and pepper to taste in a blender and blend until thoroughly mixed.
8. Remove the chops from the oven and divide them into two serving plates.
9. Serve immediately, spooning mustard mixture over chops and garnishing each dish with a mint leaf.

Nutrients Values: Fat: 6g - Carbs: 13g - Protein: 2g - Calories: 99

6.17 Old Lamb Granny Burger

PREP TIME: 10 Minutes

COOK TIME: 20 minutes

SERVES: 4 servings

DIFFICULTY LEVEL: Easy

INGREDIENTS:

- 1 pound lamb breast, freshly ground
- 4 garlic cloves, peeled and chopped
- 1 egg, whole
- ¼ cup plain bread crumbs
- 1 tin (14 ounces) small chopped diced tomatoes with jalapeno peppers, thoroughly drained
- To taste, season with salt and freshly ground pepper

DIRECTIONS

1. Preheat the broiler in the oven.
2. Mix lamb, garlic, eggs, well-drained tomatoes (place tomatoes in a strainer and press down with a heavy spoon to squeeze out enough liquid as feasible), bread crumbs, and salt and pepper in a large mixing bowl.
3. Mix the ingredients in a large mixing bowl and shape them into four patties.
4. Place patties 4 inches below the broiler on a baking sheet.
5. Broil for 15–20 minutes on each side, or until tops are crispy and juices flow clear when fork pierced.
6. As desired, garnish.

Nutrients Values: Fat: 14g - Carbs: 5g - Protein: 8g - Calories: 200

6.18 Pan-Grilled Minced Pork Burgers

PREP TIME: 10 Minutes

COOK TIME: 5 minutes

SERVES: 4 servings

DIFFICULTY LEVEL: Moderate

INGREDIENTS:

- Cooking spray with canola oil
- 1 ½ pound ground pork that is fresh and lean
- 4 scallions, chopped (white and green portions)
- A quarter teaspoon of garlic powder
- ½ tbsp. paprika
- ¼ teaspoon cayenne pepper
- To taste freshly ground pepper
- 1 tablespoon capers, chopped
- Garnish with raw onion & stone-ground mustard

DIRECTIONS

1. Coat a curved grill pan using cooking oil and place it on the stovetop.

2. Preheat the pan over high heat on the stovetop.

3. Mix the pork, scallions, spices, and capers in a mixing bowl.

4. Make four patties out of the mixture.

5. Place patties in a heated grill pan, lower heat to medium-high, and cook for 4–5 minutes on each side or till juices run clear, turning burgers just once.

6. Serve with sliced raw onion and stone-ground mustard.

7. If preferred, once thoroughly cooked.

Nutrients Values: Protein 7g - Carbs 26g - Fat 8.9g - Fiber 4g - Calories 202

6.19 Pork & Marsala Wine

PREP TIME: 20 Minutes

COOK TIME: 10 minutes

SERVES: 4 servings

DIFFICULTY LEVEL: Easy

INGREDIENTS:

- 6 boneless pork chops, thinly sliced (cut into ¼ -inch chunks)
- To taste, season with salt and freshly ground pepper
- A quarter cup of all-purpose flour (distributed)
- 3 tablespoons canola/olive oil spread (trans fat–free), split
- 1 tablespoon extra virgin olive oil
- 8 oz. quartered button mushrooms
- 1 finely sliced tiny white onion
- A third of a cup of sweet Marsala wine
- ½ cup fat-free, low-sodium chicken broth from a can
- 2 tsp lemon juice, freshly squeezed
- 1 tablespoon fresh parsley, chopped
- Pasta of your choice

DIRECTIONS

1. Chops should be rinsed in cold water and dried with paper towels.

2. Combine three tablespoons of flour, salt, and pepper in a small bowl.

3. Dredge the pork chops in the flour mixture and shake off any extra flour.

4. In a large pan, over medium flame, heat two tablespoons of canola/olive oil.

5. Cook until the chops are browned, approximately 2 minutes on each side.

6. Place on a platter and cover with foil to keep warm.

7. In the same skillet, melt the remaining spread and add the mushrooms, onion, and salt & pepper to taste.

8. Cook for 8 minutes, or until the mushrooms are tender and golden.

9. One minute after adding the remaining flour, stir to combine.

10. Cook, constantly whisking, until the Marsala and broth have slightly thickened, about 2 minutes.

11. Allow it to simmer until the pork chunks, juices from the dish, lime juice, and parsley are cooked through, and the flavors have blended.

12. Serve over spaghetti that has been cooked.

Nutrients Values: Fat 10.5g - Protein 6g - Carbs 49g - `Fiber 8g - Calories 280

6.20 Pork chops with Sage

PREP TIME: 20 Minutes

COOK TIME: 30 minutes

SERVES: 4 servings

DIFFICULTY LEVEL: Easy

INGREDIENTS:

- 2 tbsp flour (all-purpose)
- 1 tablespoon fresh sage, chopped
- 2 tbsp. canola/olive oil spread (no trans fats)
- 4 bone-in pork chops (96 ounces) with extra fat removed
- 2 tbsp flour (all-purpose)
- 2 tablespoons extra virgin olive oil
- To taste, season with salt and freshly ground pepper.
- 2 tbsp. white wine (for deglazing)

DIRECTIONS

1. On a big, low-rimmed dish, mix flour, sage, and salt and pepper to taste.
2. Using the flour mixture, coat both sides of each pork chop.
3. In a large skillet, combine olive oil and canola/olive oil spread and heat over medium-high heat.
4. Cook for 6–7 minutes on each side, or until pork chops are fully cooked; lower heat to a low simmer.
5. Transfer pork ribs to a hot platter using a big slotted spatula.
6. To make a deglazed sauce, pour wine into the skillet and scrape off any bits from the bottom.
7. Serve the pork chops with the deglazed sauce.

Nutrients Values: Protein 13.4g -Fat 25g- Carbs 7g- Fiber 5g -Net carbs 2g -Calories 312g

6.21 Meatloaf Of Lamb

PREP TIME: 20 Minutes

COOK TIME: 30 minutes

SERVES: 8 servings

DIFFICULTY LEVEL: Moderate

INGREDIENTS:

- 3 garlic cloves, peeled and chopped
- ½ teaspoon pepper, freshly ground
- ½ cup white onion, chopped
- ½ cup carrots, chopped
- ½ cup celery, chopped
- 2 big beaten eggs
- Season with salt to taste
- 1 ½ tsp. Worcestershire sauce
- 1 tablespoon extra virgin olive oil
- Cooking spray with olive oil
- 1/3 cup fat-free, low-sodium chicken broth from a can
- 3 oz. tomato puree
- ¾ cup bread crumbs (Italian style)
- Ground lamb weighing 134 pounds

DIRECTIONS

1. Preheat the oven to 375 degrees Fahrenheit.
2. In a medium pan, heat the olive oil over medium-high heat.
3. Sauté the garlic and onion until they are tender and aromatic.
4. Cook until the carrots and celery are tender, then season with salt and pepper.
5. Combine the Worcestershire sauce, broth, tomato paste, and eggs in a mixing bowl.
6. Allow cooling slightly.
7. Place the mixture in a mixing basin and stir in the bread crumbs and ground lamb. Combine all of the ingredients well.
8. Cooking oil should be sprayed inside a 9x13 inch loaf pan.
9. Spread out the turkey mixture equally in a loaf pan.
10. Bake for 1 hour, or until a meat thermometer inserted into the middle registers 170°F.
11. Before serving, remove from the oven and set aside for 5 minutes.

NUTRIENTS VALUES: PROTEIN 10G - CARBS 18G - FAT 80G - FIBER 5G - NET CARBS 13G - CALORIES 900

6.22 Tetrazzini Of Beef

PREP TIME: 20 Minutes

COOK TIME: 30 minutes

SERVES: 8 servings

DIFFICULTY LEVEL: Easy

INGREDIENTS:

- Cooking spray with olive oil
- ½ cup Parmesan cheese, grated, divided
- 3 cups fat-free, low-sodium chicken broth from a can
- spaghetti (1 pound)
- ½ cup canola/olive oil spread with no trans fats
- 2 quarts of fat-free milk
- 8 oz. peas, frozen
- ½ cup flour, All-purpose
- 4 cups cooked turkey meat, chopped paprika to be used as a garnish

DIRECTIONS

1. Preheat the oven to 350 degrees Fahrenheit.
2. Using cooking oil, lightly coat the interior of an oven-safe casserole dish.
3. Cook pasta according to package directions in a large saucepan of boiling water.
4. Drain the pasta and place it in a casserole dish.
5. Melt the canola/olive oil and spread in a saucepan over medium heat.
6. Mix in the flour until it's completely smooth.
7. Pour in the broth, milk, and peas.
8. Cook, constantly stirring, until it reaches a boil.
9. Remove the mixture from the heat and stir in 1 ¼ cups Parmesan cheese.
10. Stir in the beef meat, then pour the mixture over the spaghetti.

11. Toss well to combine, then top with the remaining cheese and paprika.

12. Place in the oven for 1 hour or until the top is gently browned.

Nutrients Values: Fat7.5g - Protein 6g; Carbs 74g - Fiber 10.6g - Calories362

6.23 Liver With Apple & Shallots

PREP TIME: 10 Minutes

COOK TIME: 25 minutes

SERVES: 2 servings

DIFFICULTY LEVEL: Easy

INGREDIENTS:

- 2 tbsp butter (unsalted)
- 1/2 pound onion
- 2 apples, Granny Smith
- 2 tbsp. currants (dry)
- A quarter-cup of white wine
- 1 tbsp. freshly squeezed lemon juice
- 1 tbsp. balsamic vinegar
- 1 teaspoon of brown sugar
- 1 quart of water
- 1 tablespoon fresh rosemary, plus a few stems for decoration
- 8 oz. liver of a calf
- 1/4 teaspoon salt
- Spray with extra virgin olive oil
- Spritz with olive oil

DIRECTIONS

1. Preheat the oven to 200 degrees Fahrenheit.

2. Set a pan over medium heat and coat with extra virgin olive oil spray; put onions and saute for approximately four minutes, or until transparent.

3. Cook for approximately five minutes, or until the apples begin to brown.

4. Cook till apples are soft, stirring in water, lime juice, vinegar, and sugar.

5. Stir in the rosemary and currants, simmer for approximately 2 minutes while stirring constantly, then divide over two dishes and keep warm in the oven.

6. In the same pan, melt the butter until it foams.

7. Stir in the liver and cook for approximately 10 minutes or until the exterior is browned.

8. Distribute the liver amongst the two apple-onion plates. To deglaze the pan, add white wine and simmer till the liquid is dropped by half, then pour equal quantities over each dish. Serve with a sprig of fresh rosemary on top.

Nutrients Values: Fat 11.8g - Protein 10g - Carbs 58g - Fiber 9.1g - Calories 331

6.24 Lamb Chops

PREP TIME: 10 Minutes

COOK TIME: 10 minutes

SERVES: 4 servings

DIFFICULTY LEVEL: Moderate

INGREDIENTS:

- 1 tbsp. minced garlic
- 1/4 teaspoon freshly ground black pepper
- Spray for cooking
- 1/2 tbsp. salt
- 2 tbsp lemon juice, freshly squeezed
- 1 tbsp. oregano, dry
- 8 fat-trimmed lamb loin chops

DIRECTIONS

1. Preheat the oven to broil.
2. Combine all of the spices, herbs, and lemon juice in a small dish and rub the mix on each side of the lamb chops.
3. Grill the lamb chops for four minutes on every side or until done to your liking on a broiler pan sprayed with cooking spray.
4. Cover the grilled lamb chops with foil and set aside for five minutes before serving.

Nutrients Values: Fat 4.3g - Protein 18g - Carbs 59g - Fiber 12.9g - Calories 310

6.25 Seared Calf's Liver

PREP TIME: 20 Minutes

COOK TIME: 10 minutes

SERVES: 4 servings

DIFFICULTY LEVEL: Easy

INGREDIENTS:

- 2 tsp olive oil (extra virgin)
- 2 tablespoons red wine
- 8 ounces of calves' liver, sliced into thin strips one garlic clove, minced
- 1 tablespoon parsley (flat-leaf)
- 1 tbsp. sage (fresh)
- Peppercorns
- 2 tbsp butter (unsalted)
- 1 teaspoon lemon juice
- One tsp balsamic vinaigrette
- 1/4 teaspoon salt

DIRECTIONS

1. Heat extra virgin olive oil in a nonstick pan over medium heat; add minced garlic and cook for three minutes, or until transparent and aromatic.

2. Cook for approximately five minutes, or until the meat is charred on the exterior, adding liver, parsley, and sage strips as needed.

3. Transfer the liver to a heated dish and deglaze the pan for approximately thirty seconds with vinegar, red wine, butter, & lime juice.

4. Serve immediately after pouring the sauce on the meat.

Nutrients Values: Protein 13g - Carbs 1.3g - Fat 22g - Fiber 0g - Calories 257

6.26 Broccoli With Chicken

PREP TIME: 5 Minutes

COOK TIME: 20 minutes

SERVES: 4 servings

DIFFICULTY LEVEL: Easy

INGREDIENTS:

- 1 tbsp. vegetable oil, split
- 1 finely sliced green onion
- ½ cup broccoli florets
- 2 ½ tbsp. corn starch
- ½ cup soy sauce
- ½ cup water
- 1/2 shallots, cut finely
- 1 small garlic clove, minced
- ½ Pound finely cut chicken steak
- 1 tsp red pepper flakes, crushed
- 1 tbsp. fresh ginger, minced
- Honey, 2 tbsp.

DIRECTIONS

1. In a medium-sized skillet, heat the oil.

2. Cook for about eight minutes, or until the chicken is browned.

3. Set the steak aside after removing it from the pan.

4. In the same pan, sauté the green onions, shallots, and garlic for one minute, stirring constantly.

5. Cook for five minutes after adding the broccoli.

6. In a mixing basin, whisk together cornstarch and water until smooth.

7. Combine the red pepper flakes, ginger, honey, and soy sauce in a separate dish; whisk in the cornstarch mixture until thoroughly mixed.

8. Cook for about five minutes or until the sauce has thickened.

9. Cook for three minutes after adding the chicken.

10. Over brown rice, serve.

Nutrients Values: Fat: 1g - Carbs: 24g - Protein: 0g - Calories: 108

6.27 Pork Curry with Olives, Apricots,& Cauliflower

PREP TIME: 15 Minutes

COOK TIME: 8 minutes

SERVES: 6 servings

DIFFICULTY LEVEL: Easy

INGREDIENTS:

- 8 skinless, boneless pork thighs
- 1 cauliflower head, chopped
- ½ tsp. powdered cinnamon
- ¼ teaspoon cayenne
- 1 tbsp. Apple cider vinegar
- 1 tsp. smoky paprika split to taste with sea salt
- ¼ cup extra virgin olive oil, split
- 1 cup pitted green olives, halved
- 4 tsp. curry powder
- ¾ cup dried apricots, diced, steeped in boiling water, and drained
- 1/3 cup fresh cilantro, chopped
- 6 slices of lemon

DIRECTIONS

1. In a medium bowl, combine two tablespoons, of extra virgin olive oil, cinnamon, cayenne, the pork thighs, ½ teaspoon of paprika, vinegar, two tablespoons of curry powder, and sea salt; toss to coat, and chill for about 8 hours, covered.

2. Preheat the oven to 4500F and place the rack in the center.

3. Line a rimmed sheet pan with parchment paper; combine cauliflower, remaining olive oil, paprika, and curry powder in a large mixing bowl.

4. Pour the ingredients into a single layer with the olives and apricots.

5. Place the marinated pork on top of the cauliflower mixture, equally spaced, and roast for 35 minutes, or until the chicken is cooked through and the cauliflower has browned.

6. Serve the cauliflower and pork with cilantro and lemon wedges on the side.

Nutrients Values: Fat 2.3 g – Protein 15g – Carbs 48g – Fiber 11.8 g - Calories 246

6.28 Brussels Sprouts Creamy Soup

PREP TIME: 15 Minutes

COOK TIME: 10 minutes

SERVES: 4 servings

DIFFICULTY LEVEL: Easy

INGREDIENTS:

- 4 tablespoons trans-fat–free canola/olive oil spread one white onion, chopped
- 1 large leek, thinly sliced white parts and sliced green parts, keep separate
- 4 cloves fresh garlic, minced
- 8 ounces fresh brussels sprouts, sliced
- 1 teaspoon ground coriander
- 5 ounces fresh green beans, thinly sliced
- Five cups of low-sodium, fat-free vegetable broth
- 1½ cups frozen peas, defrosted
- 1 cup of low-fat milk
- 4 teaspoons all-purpose flour
- Salt and freshly ground pepper
- 1 tablespoon freshly squeezed lemon juice
- To taste herb-flavored croutons for garnish

DIRECTIONS

1. Melt the canola/olive oil over low heat in a large skillet.
2. Add the onion and garlic and roast until tender and fragrant, but not brown.
3. Add to the pan the green pieces of the leek, the brussels sprouts, and the green beans.
4. Stir in the broth and get it to a boil.
5. Reduce the heat and leave for 10 minutes to simmer.
6. Add the peas, lemon juice, and coriander and boil for 10-15 minutes or until the vegetables are tender.
7. Remove the vegetable mixture from the heat and cool slowly, then switch it to a food processor or blender and process until smooth.
8. Bringing the white pieces of the leek back into the saucepan.
9. Bring over medium-high heat to a boil, reduce to a simmer for around 5 minutes, and reduce to stay warm again.
10. Whisk together the milk and flour in a separate, shallow bowl until smooth.
11. Add flour
12. Combine with the soup, bring to a simmer, and add salt and pepper to taste.
13. If chosen, serve with a sprinkle of croutons on top.

Nutrients Values: Protein 18g – Carbs 58g – Fat 99g – Fiber 13g - Calories 363

6.29 Raisins, Garbanzos, and Spinach Pasta

PREP TIME: 15 Minutes

COOK TIME: 25 minutes

SERVES: 6 servings

DIFFICULTY LEVEL: Easy

INGREDIENTS:

- 4 cups fresh spinach, chopped
- Farfalle (bow-tie) pasta, 8 oz.
- 2 tbsp. Parmigiano-Reggiano black peppercorns, cracked
- 4 smashed garlic cloves
- ½ cup broth de poulet (unsalted)
- ½ (19 oz.) washed and drained garbanzo beans
- 2 tbsp olive oil (extra virgin)
- ½ cup raisin golden

DIRECTIONS

1. Fill a saucepan three full with salted water and bring to a boil over high heat.
2. Cook for 12 minutes, or until pasta is al dente; drain and put aside.
3. In a large pan, heat extra virgin olive oil and sauté garlic till fragrant; pour chicken broth and beans and mix to cook thoroughly.
4. Cook for 3 minutes, or until spinach is wilted, after adding the spinach and raisins. Distribute the pasta among the dishes and top with approximately a sixth sauce, peppercorns, and Parmesan cheese.
5. Serve immediately.

Nutrients Values: Fat 0.7g– Protein 6.2g – Carbs 3g – Fiber 9g – Calories 153

6.30 Eggplant Steak with Feta Cheese, Black Olives, Roasted Peppers, and Chickpeas

PREP TIME: 20 Minutes

COOK TIME: 10 minutes

SERVES: 4 servings

DIFFICULTY LEVEL: Easy

INGREDIENTS:

- Marinade with balsamic vinegar
- 2 garlic cloves, minced
- 1 tbsp. tamari (low-sodium)
- 1 tablespoon balsamic vinaigrette
- ¼ tsp. black pepper, freshly ground
- 2 tbsp olive oil (extra virgin)

- Steaks of Eggplant
- ¼ pound crumbled feta cheese
- 1 big eggplant, around 1 pound
- ½ cup drained chickpeas
- Two chopped roasted red peppers
- balsamic vinegar, 4 tsp.
- Oregano, a pinch
- ½ cup black olives pitted salt from the sea
- black pepper, freshly ground
- 4 pita bread (6 ½ -inch circular)
- Garnish with fresh oregano

DIRECTIONS

Marinade:

1. Combine the marinade ingredients in a bowl and mix in the extra virgin olive oil until thoroughly blended.
2. Remove from the equation.
3. Preheat the grill or broiler.
4. Cut the eggplant lengthwise into four ¼ -inch thick slices to resemble steaks.
5. Brush the marinade over the eggplant slices and broil or grill for 2 minutes a side, or until cooked.
6. One by one, place the grilled eggplants on the plates.
7. Mix feta, red peppers, chickpeas, oregano, and black olives in a small mixing bowl; season with sea salt and crushed black pepper.
8. Stir in some of the marinades until everything is thoroughly combined.
9. Pita bread should be grilled or toasted and sliced into wedges before serving.
10. Drizzle balsamic vinegar over the eggplant "steak" and ladle roughly two scoops of the olive-pepper mix on top.
11. Sprinkle with oregano sprigs and a couple of pita bread slices.
12. Continue with the rest of the ingredients and serve right away.

Nutrients Values: Fat 7.4g – Protein 16g – Carbs 56g – Fiber 12g – Calories 322

6.31 Chicken Penne Pasta

PREP TIME: 20 Minutes

COOK TIME: 30 minutes

SERVES: 4 servings

DIFFICULTY LEVEL: Easy

INGREDIENTS:

- One pound of penne pasta
- ½ tablespoons butter
- ½ cup chopped red onion
- Two garlic cloves, squeezed
- ¾ kg deboned and skinned chicken breasts, split in half
- ½ cup feta cheese, crumbled
- One tin artichoke heart, soaking in water
- lemon juice, two tbsp.
- One chopped tomato
- Three tbsp. chopped fresh parsley
- Sea Salt
- Black pepper, freshly ground
- One teaspoon of dried oregano

DIRECTIONS

1. In a large pot with salted boiling water, cook the penne pasta until al dente.
2. In a large skillet over medium heat, melt the butter and add the onions and garlic.
3. Cook for 2 minutes before adding the chicken.
4. For about 6 minutes, stir regularly until the chicken is golden brown.
5. Drain the artichoke hearts and combine them with the cheese, lemon juice, tomatoes, oregano, parsley, and drained pasta in a pan.
6. Reduce the heat to low and continue to cook for another 3 minutes.
7. Season with salt and pepper to taste, and serve immediately.

Nutrients Values: Fat 2.3 g – Protein 15g – Carbs 48g – Fiber 11.8 g - Calories 246

6.32 Greek Chicken & Beans

PREP TIME: 10 Minutes

COOK TIME: 50 minutes

SERVES: 6 servings

DIFFICULTY LEVEL: Easy

INGREDIENTS:

- 2 skinless, boneless chicken legs (3 ounces)
- 2 onions, big chunks chopped
- 5 carrots, one sliced, the others chopped into big chunks
- 2 skinless, boneless chicken breasts (4 oz.)
- Cooking spray with olive oil
- 2 peeled tomatoes, cut into big chunks
- 2 cups fat-free, low-sodium chicken broth from a can

- 4c. canned goods drained and washed beans
- 2 tbsp. fresh parsley, chopped
- 12 green bell peppers, cut into big chunks
- 2 celery stalks, 1 chopped and the other diced into large chunks
- 2 tsp. thyme (fresh)
- To taste, season with salt and freshly ground pepper
- 3 garlic cloves, peeled and chopped

DIRECTIONS

1. Rinse the chicken and pat it dry.
2. Combine the chicken, half of the onions, one sliced carrot, and one cut celery stalk in a saucepan.
3. Cook until the chicken is cooked, adding enough water to cover the meat.
4. Set aside after straining.
5. Using cooking spray, lightly coat the sides and bottom of a big casserole dish, then put chicken 2 cups of stock, and beans.
6. Toss in the remaining carrot and celery pieces with the tomatoes, thyme, remaining onions, green bell pepper, parsley, garlic, and salt and pepper in the casserole.
7. Bake for approximately 45 minutes or until the mixture has reached a simmer.
8. Serve immediately.

Nutrients Values: Fat: 1g - Protein: 4g - Carbs: 34g- Calories: 159

6.33 Chicken & Eggplant

PREP TIME: 30 Minutes

COOK TIME: 45 minutes

SERVES: 8 servings

DIFFICULTY LEVEL: Moderate

INGREDIENTS:

- 2 medium peeled eggplants, cut into 1 ½ -inch cubes
- ½ cup extra-virgin olive oil + 2 teaspoons extra-virgin olive oil, divided
- 3-pound chicken, skinless and boneless
- 2 big sliced onions
- 4 garlic cloves, peeled and chopped
- 1 teaspoon spice mixture

Mix Spices

- 2 tsp. thick pomegranate juice tablespoons
- 2 tsp allspice powder
- 1 teaspoon cinnamon powder

- 1 teaspoon cilantro, chopped
- 1 teaspoon cumin powder
- ¼ teaspoon pepper, freshly ground
- 1 teaspoon clove powder
- 4 big peeled, seeded, and chopped tomatoes
- 2 tablespoons fresh parsley, freshly chopped
- Freshly squeezed lemon juice
- To taste, season with salt and freshly ground pepper

DIRECTIONS

1. Salt the eggplant slices thoroughly and drain for 30 minutes in a strainer (this rids the eggplant of its bitter juices).
2. After 30 minutes, rinse the pieces under cold running water, gently wring the excess moisture out with your hands, then pat dry using paper towels.
3. Half cup olive oil, heated in a big heavy pan over medium heat.
4. Sauté half of an eggplant slice until golden brown, flipping often.
5. Put pieces on paper towels for draining and absorb excess oil with a slotted spoon.
6. Continue cooking the remaining eggplant, using additional olive oil as needed.
7. Remove the olive oil from the skillet, set it aside to cool, and then wipe it clean.
8. Clean the chicken pieces by rinsing them in cold water and patting them dry using paper towels.
9. Place the chicken in a pan with two tablespoons of olive oil and cook until golden brown on both sides.
10. Place the pieces on a platter.
11. All but three tablespoons of drippings should be poured out of the skillet.
12. Over medium heat, add the onions and cook until golden brown.
13. Sauté for 30 seconds, constantly stirring, after adding the garlic and seasonings. Toss in the tomato, thick pomegranate molasses, and lime juice, and season to taste with salt and pepper.
14. Transfer the chicken to the skill and any juices from the dish, and pour the tomato mixture around the pieces.
15. Bring to a boil, then turn down to low heat.
16. Cover and cook for 45 minutes, or till chicken is cooked through.
17. Add the sautéed eggplant and parsley, covered it, and continue to cook for another 10 minutes.
18. Season with salt and pepper to taste.
19. Serve with a spaghetti side dish.

Nutrients Values: Fat: 2.9g - Protein: 4g - Carbs: 55g - Fiber: 9.6g - Calories: 233

6.34 Spicy Chicken With Couscous

PREP TIME: 20 Minutes

COOK TIME: 30 minutes

SERVES: 4 servings

DIFFICULTY LEVEL: Easy

INGREDIENTS:

- ¼ teaspoon cumin powder
- ¼ teaspoon turmeric powder
- 1 teaspoon cayenne pepper, ground
- 1 pound chicken breasts, skinless and boneless, cut into 1-inch strips
- 1 tbsp extra-virgin olive oil
- 5 fresh garlic cloves, coarsely minced
- 1 (16-ounce) tin of fat-free, low-sodium chicken broth
- 1cup peas, fresh one big sliced white onion
- 1 medium chopped red bell pepper
- To taste, season with salt and freshly ground pepper
- ¼ cup finely chopped cilantro, for garnish
- 1 cup couscous

DIRECTIONS

1. Sprinkle the turmeric, cumin, and cayenne pepper equally over the chicken pieces and leave them aside.
2. Heat the olive oil in a nonstick saucepan over medium heat until it is hot.
3. Cook, occasionally stirring, for 3 minutes, or until the chicken is golden brown.
4. In a pan, combine stock, peas, onion, red bell pepper, salt, and pepper to taste; bring to a boil, reduce heat to low, and cook for 2–3 minutes, or until chicken is cooked through.
5. Stir in the couscous, cover, and set aside.
6. Allow setting until the liquid has been absorbed.
7. Serve with cilantro as a garnish.

Nutrients Values: Fat 5.1g - Protein 18g – Carbs 53g –Fiber 11g - Calories 305

6.35 Chicken With Pomegranate Sauce

PREP TIME: 20 Minutes

COOK TIME: 30 minutes

SERVES: 8 servings

DIFFICULTY LEVEL: Easy

INGREDIENTS:

- 4-pound chicken breast, skinless and boneless, cut into tiny pieces
- paprika, 2 tablespoons
- To taste, season with salt and freshly ground pepper.
- ¼ cup extra-virgin olive oil
- 4 fresh garlic cloves, minced
- ¼ cup chopped fresh parsley
- 2 medium yellow onions, chopped
- 1 coarsely chopped tiny spicy banana pepper
- 3 teaspoons of oil Pomegranate Molasses, Thick
- 4 cups chunky tomatoes in a can, undrained

DIRECTIONS

1. Chicken should be washed, fat removed, and chopped into tiny pieces.
2. Season with salt and pepper, and paprika.
3. In a saucepan, heat the olive oil, then add the chicken pieces and stir-fry for 2–3 minutes.
4. Stir in the garlic for further 2–3 minutes.
5. Cover and bring to a boil with the onions, parsley, hot banana pepper, Thick Pomegranate Molasses, and tomatoes with liquid.
6. Cook for 30 minutes over medium-low heat or until the chicken is cooked.
7. Serve with a side of rice.

Nutrients Values: Fat 5.9g - Protein 11g - Carbs 24g - Fiber 5g - Calories 171

CHAPTER 7: DINNER RECIPES FOR INTERMITTENT FASTING

While doing intermittent fasting, these are the simple dinner meals you will make again and again. There is something for everyone with various healthy, easy, chicken, vegetarian, and budget-friendly recipe ideas. Bon appetite!

7.1 Mediterranean chicken breast with avocado tapenade

PREP TIME: 15 Minutes

COOK TIME: 5 minutes

SERVES: 4 servings

DIFFICULTY LEVEL: Easy

INGREDIENTS:

- 1 tbsp of grated lemon peel
- 4 skinless and boneless chicken breast halves
- 2 tbsp of olive oil
- 5 tbsp of fresh lemon juice
- 1 finely chopped garlic clove
- ¼ teaspoon of ground black pepper
- ½ teaspoon salt

- 2 roasted and mashed garlic cloves
- ¼ fresh ground pepper
- ½ teaspoon sea salt
- 1 seeded and finely chopped medium tomato
- 3 tbsp of rinsed capers
- ¼ thinly sliced cup of small green pimento-stuffed olive
- 1 finely chopped Hass avocado
- 2 tbsp of finely sliced fresh basil leaves

DIRECTIONS:

1. In a sealable plastic bag, combine chicken, two tablespoons of lemon juice, lemon peel, olive oil, salt, garlic, and pepper. Refrigerate for approximately 30 minutes after sealing the bag.

2. Combine the remaining three teaspoons of lemon juice, 1/2 teaspoon olive oil, sea salt, roasted garlic, and freshly ground pepper in a mixing bowl. Mix the basil, green olives, tomato capers, and avocado and set them aside.

3. Remove the chicken from the bag and pour out the marinade. Grill for about 4 to 5 minutes per side over medium-hot coals or until the optimal degree of doneness is achieved.

4. Avocado Tapenade is a great addition to serve with this dish.

7.2 Vegan lentil burgers

PREP TIME: 1 hour 10 Minutes

COOK TIME: 20 minutes

SERVES: 4 servings

DIFFICULTY LEVEL: Easy

INGREDIENTS:

- 2 ½ cups water
- 1 cup well rinsed dry lentils
- ½ teaspoon salt
- ½ diced onion
- 1 tbsp of olive oil
- 1 diced carrot
- 1 tbsp of soy sauce
- 1 teaspoon pepper
- ¾ cup finely ground rolled oats
- ¾ cup breadcrumbs

DIRECTIONS:

1. Lentils should be cooked for 45 minutes in salted water. The lentils would be soft, and much of the moisture would have evaporated.
2. In a small amount of oil, fry the onions and carrots until tender, approximately for 5 minutes.
3. Combine the cooked ingredients, soy sauce, pepper, oats, and breadcrumbs in a bowl.
4. Shape the mixture into patties when it is still warm; it will produce 8-10 burgers.
5. After that, the burgers can be shallow fried for about 1-2 minutes on each side or baked for 15 minutes at 200°C.

7.3 Brussel sprout and sheet pan chicken

PREP TIME: 40 Minutes

COOK TIME: 30 minutes

SERVES: 4 servings

DIFFICULTY LEVEL: Easy

INGREDIENTS:

- ½ cup Brussels sprouts
- 4 skin-on chicken thighs
- 3 tbsp of olive oil
- 4 carrots, cut on the bias
- 1 tbsp of herb de Provence

DIRECTIONS:

1. Preheat the oven to 400 degrees Fahrenheit.
2. Put 11/2 tbsp olive oil, 12 tsp herbs, pepper, and salt in a bowl and add the cut vegetables. Rub the vegetables all over.
3. Arrange the vegetables on a sheet pan.
4. In the same bowl, place the chicken thighs. Drizzle with 1/2 tablespoons of herbs, and 1/12 tablespoons olive oil, and season with salt and pepper. Rub the chicken all over.
5. Place the chicken in the pan.
6. Roast for 30-35 minutes, or until chicken is cooked through.
7. Switch the oven to broil and roast for a minute or two and if you want a crispier chicken skin or crispier vegetable. If you do not keep an eye on it, it can burn, so watch carefully.

7.4 Crockpot black-eyed peas

PREP TIME: 1 hour 5 Minutes

COOK TIME: 10 minutes

SERVES: 6 servings

DIFFICULTY LEVEL: Easy

INGREDIENTS:

- 1 bag of 16oz dried black-eyed peas
- 1 small ham hock
- 1 can of Del Monte zesty jalapeno pepper
- 1 can of diced tomato with green chilies
- 2 cans of chicken broth 1 chopped stalk of celery

DIRECTIONS:

1. Pre-soak the black-eyed peas according to the instructions given in the bag.
2. Mix all the ingredients and cook on a low medium flame for about 1 hour.
3. Serve with white rice.

7.5 Brocolli dal curry

PREP TIME: 1 hour 30 Minutes

COOK TIME: 45 minutes

SERVES: 4 servings

DIFFICULTY LEVEL: Moderate

INGREDIENTS:

- 4tbsp of butter or 4 tbsp of ghee
- 2 chopped onions
- 1 tbsp of chili powder
- 1 ½ teaspoon of black pepper
- 2 tbsp of cumin
- 1 teaspoon ground coriander
- 2 teaspoons turmeric
- 1 cup red lentil
- Juice of a lemon
- 3 cups chicken broth
- 2 finely chopped medium broccoli
- ½ cup dried coconut
- 1 tbsp of flour
- 1 teaspoon of salt
- 1 cup of coarsely chopped cashews

DIRECTIONS:

1. In a saucepan, melt the butter and brown the onions.
2. Now add the pepper, chili powder, cumin, coriander, and turmeric.
3. And stir and cook for a minute.
4. Add the lemon juice, lentils, broth, and coconut.
5. Bring to a boil, reduce to low heat, and cook for 45-55 minutes (if the mixture becomes thick, you have to add a little hot water).
6. Now steam the broccoli for approximately 7min.
7. Set aside broccoli after submerging it in cool water.
8. Remove 1/3 cup of the liquid from the lentil mixture.
9. To make a smooth paste, add the flour.
10. Return it to the pan and mix in the salt, broccoli, and nuts.
11. Cook for 5 minutes on low heat.
12. Serve with basmati rice.

7.6 Stuffed Sesame Chicken Breasts

PREP TIME: 5 minutes

COOK TIME: 16 minutes

SERVES: 4 servings

DIFFICULTY LEVEL: Easy

INGREDIENTS:

- ¼ coarsely chopped tiny red chili pepper
- A quarter cup of sesame seeds
- A quarter-cup of lime juice
- 4 skinless, b1less chicken breasts (4–5 ounces)
- 4 sprigs of fresh tarragon for garnish
- 4 sprigs of fresh tarragon or 1 tablespoon dried tarragon
- Sprinkle with extra-virgin olive oil
- To taste, season with salt and freshly ground pepper.
- 12 deseeded and thinly sliced green bell pepper
- 12 deseeded and thinly sliced red bell pepper

DIRECTIONS

1. Using paper towels, gently dry the breasts after rinsing them under cold water.
2. Split apart 1 side of the breasts with a sharp knife to make a pocket.
3. Season the insides of the breasts with salt and pepper as desired, as well as tarragon (1 tablespoon dried tarragon for each breast or 1 whole sprig tucked into each breast pocket).
4. Fill each breast pocket with green and red bell pepper slices, then seal and secure with a toothpick.
5. Set aside the lime juice and chile pepper.

6. Sprinkle many sesame seeds over each breast and arrange them in a single layer on a nonstick baking sheet.
7. Drizzle the lime/chili mixture over the tops of the breasts and bake for 30 minutes at 400 degrees, or until the chicken is juicy and cooked through.
8. Preheat the oven to broil and sprinkle a little olive oil over each breast.
9. Broil the chicken breasts on a baking pan until the sesame seeds are nicely browned.
10. Serve with fresh tarragon sprigs on top.

Nutrients Values: Fat: 14g - Carbs: 9g - Protein: 1g – Fiber 103mg - Calories: 159

7.7 Fillets Of Broiled Chicken Breast & Mango

PREP TIME: 5 minutes

COOK TIME: 16 minutes

SERVES: 4 servings

DIFFICULTY LEVEL: Easy

INGREDIENTS:

- 4 big, crushed bay leaves
- 4 skinless, b1less chicken breast fillets (4–5 ounces)
- 1 tbsp extra-virgin olive oil
- 6 big pitted black olives halved
- 3 tablespoons dry cream sherry
- To taste, season with salt and freshly ground pepper.
- 2 peeled and cut into wedges ripe but firm mangos
- 2 teaspoons fresh garlic, coarsely chopped

DIRECTIONS

1. Fillets should be rinsed in cold water and dried with paper towels.
2. In a shallow baking dish, arrange the steaks in a single layer.
3. Season the tops of the steaks with salt and pepper to taste.
4. Over the fillets, strew bay leaves, olives, and garlic.
5. Mix sherry and olive oil in a small bowl.
6. Drizzle over fillets after whisking to combine flavors.
7. Mango wedges should be strewn over and around the fillets.
8. Preheat the oven to 350°F and bake the fillets for 8–10 minutes, or until juices flow clear when probed with a fork.
9. Preheat the oven to broil.
10. Transfer baking tray to top shelf of oven and roast tops of steaks until nicely browned, approximately 4 inches from the flame.
11. Served, hot, drizzled with the liquids from the baking dish, and garnished with mango slices.

Nutrients Values: Fat: 1g - Protein: 4g - Carbs: 34g- Calories: 159

7.8 Turkey With Black Olives

PREP TIME: 5 minutes

COOK TIME: 16 minutes

SERVES 4: servings

DIFFICULTY LEVEL: Easy

INGREDIENTS:

- ½ teaspoon rosemary (dried)
- fresh parsley, 1–2 sprigs
- 1 cup white wine (dry)
- 3 garlic cloves, peeled and smashed
- 12 black olives pitted and halved
- 2 peeled and sliced tomatoes
- 2 tbsp extra-virgin olive oil
- 2-pound minced turkey

DIRECTIONS

1. In a large pan, heat the olive oil, add the garlic and parsley, and cook until golden brown.
2. Continue to cook, often stirring, until the turkey is browned.
3. Tomatoes, rosemary, olives, and wine are added to the pan.
4. Stir in the turkey, cover, and simmer for 3–5 minutes, or until most of the liquid has evaporated.
5. Serve with a side of rice.

Nutrients Values: Fat: 3g - Carbs: 20g - Protein: 4g - Calories: 119

7.9 Rigatoni & Minced Chicken

PREP TIME: 5 minutes

COOK TIME: 16 minutes

SERVES: 4 servings

DIFFICULTY LEVEL: Easy

INGREDIENTS:

1 ½ cup peas, frozen
2 ½ teaspoon red hot pepper flakes, crushed
3 1 onion, peeled and minced
4 1 pound ground chicken
5 1 pound rigatoni pasta (whole grain)
6 3 teaspoons chopped fresh mint as a garnish
7 To taste, season with salt and freshly ground pepper.
8 2 tablespoons pesto sauce (spicy, garlicky)

DIRECTIONS

1. Fry chicken, onions, and red pepper flakes in a heavy-

bottomed pot for approximately 8 minutes, or until chicken is d1, turning periodically to split up.

2. Cook for a further 2–4 minutes after adding the peas.

3. Mix in the Spicy Garlicky Pesto Sauce and season with salt & pepper to taste, then leave aside to keep warm.
4. Cook rigatoni until al dente in boiling water, drain, and mix with chicken pesto sauce.
5. Garnish with a sprig of mint.

Nutrients Values: Fat16.5g - Protein 14g - Carbs 36g - Fiber 7.8g - Calories 313

7.10 Florentine Roasted duck

PREP TIME: 5 minutes

COOK TIME: 16 minutes

SERVES: 4 servings

DIFFICULTY LEVEL: Easy

INGREDIENTS:

- ½ teaspoon rosemary (dried)
- 4 entire garlic cloves, fresh
- 4 garlic cloves, thinly sliced
- 4-pound duck loin
- 6 tbsp. red wine, hearty (do not use cooking wine)
- To taste, season with salt and freshly ground pepper
- water (approximately 5–6 teaspoons)

DIRECTIONS

1. Cut lines approximately 1/8 inches apart into the duck's skin if it hasn't previously been scored.
2. On 1 side, slit it through the meat to the b1 and put the garlic and rosemary pieces.
3. Place the meat in a roasting pan with water and wine in a 350-degree oven and press the entire garlic cloves into the scored skin.
4. Season the meat well with salt and pepper, then roast for 2–2 ½ hours, basting periodically, until the flesh is extremely soft but still juicy.
5. Serve with a selection of veggies of your choice.

Nutrients Values: Fat: 1g - Protein: 4g - Carbs: 34g- Calories: 159

7.11 Barbecued Spicy Chicken Burger

PREP TIME: 5 minutes

COOK TIME: 16 minutes

SERVES: 4 servings

DIFFICULTY LEVEL: Easy

INGREDIENTS:

- ½ cup fresh spinach, chopped
- ½ cup seas1d Italian bread crumbs
- ½ teaspoon ketchup
- ½ tsp spicy red pepper sauce
- Alfa sprouts as a garnish

- 1 pound chicken, freshly ground
- 3 scallions, finely chopped
- 2 fresh garlic cloves, coarsely chopped
- 2 whole wheat pita bread, split into 2 with pocket open

DIRECTIONS

1. Preheat the oven to broil.
2. Mix minced chicken, garlic, scallions, spinach, bread crumbs, hot pepper sauce, and Worcestershire sauce in a large mixing bowl.
3. Stir well to combine, then divide into 4 equal-sized patties.
4. Set patties on a broiler pan and place 4 inches under the broiler in the oven.
5. Broil burgers for 6 minutes on each side, flipping only once.
6. Cook until the middle of the pie is no longer pink.
7. Remove the dish from the oven.
8. Place each burger in a pita pocket and top with preferred toppings.

Nutrients Values: Fat 5.1g - Protein 18g – Carbs 53g –Fiber 11g - Calories 305

7.12 Pork Bruschetta

PREP TIME: 5 minutes

COOK TIME: 16 minutes

SERVES: 4 servings

DIFFICULTY LEVEL: Easy

INGREDIENTS:

- 1 tbsp. extra virgin olive oil, split
- Balsamic vinegar, 2 tbsp.
- Basil leaves, fresh
- Cherry tomatoes, ½ cup
- 1 pork breast, boneless and skinless
- 1 small garlic clove, minced
- 1 small sliced onion

DIRECTIONS

1. Cook the pork in half of the oil in a pan over medium heat.
2. Meanwhile, prepare the veggies and chop basil leaves into slivers.
3. Sauté the garlic and onion in the remaining oil for around 3 minutes.
4. For approximately 5 minutes, stir in the basil and tomatoes.
5. Add the vinegar and mix well.
6. Cook until the pork is well cooked, then serve with the tomato and onion mixture on top.

Nutrients Values: Fat 5.1g - Protein 18g – Carbs 53g –Fiber 11g - Calories 305

7.13 Lamb & Coconut

PREP TIME: 5 minutes

COOK TIME: 16 minutes

SERVES 4 servings

DIFFICULTY LEVEL: Easy

INGREDIENTS:

1. 1 pound boneless, skinless chicken breast
2. ½ cup shredded coconut
3. ½ cup of almond flour
4. coconut oil 2 tbsp.
5. 1 egg (small)
6. 1 tbsp. salt

DIRECTIONS

1. Mix grated coconut, almond flour, and sea salt in a mixing bowl.
2. In a second dish, whisk the egg; put the lamb into the egg, then turn in the flour mixture until well coated.
3. In a medium-sized skillet, heat the coconut oil and cook the chicken until the coating brown.
4. Place the chicken in the oven and bake for almost 10 minutes at 350°F.

7.14 Beef Burger

PREP TIME: 5 minutes

COOK TIME: 16 minutes

SERVES 4 servings

DIFFICULTY LEVEL: Easy

INGREDIENTS:

- ½ cup dry bread crumbs
- ¾ cup mint leaves, chopped
- ¾ pound ground beef
- 1/3 cup crumbled feta cheese
- 4 hamburger buns, split
- 1 cup red onion, diced
- 1 egg white (big)
- 1 red bell pepper, roasted and sliced into strips
- 1 teaspoon dried dill
- Spray for cooking
- 2 tablespoons lime juice

DIRECTIONS

1. In a mixing bowl, lightly whisk the egg white, then add the onions, mint, breadcrumb, dill, cheese, beef, and lime juice, mixing well after each addition.
2. Distribute the beef mix into 4 reasonable burger patties.
3. Cook on medium-high in a large saucepan sprayed with cooking spray.
4. Place the patties in the skillet with care and fry for 8 minutes on each side, or until d1 to your taste.
5. Arrange the patties on the cut buns and garnish with pepper strips after they've been

cooked.

Nutrients Values: Fat 5.1g - Protein 18g – Carbs 53g –Fiber 11g - Calories 305

7.15 Mutton Salad with Greek Dressing

PREP TIME: 5 minutes

COOK TIME: 16 minutes

SERVES 4 servings

DIFFICULTY LEVEL: Easy

INGREDIENTS:

- ¼ tsp. Freshly ground pepper
- ¼ tsp. sea salt
- ½ cup feta cheese, crumbled
- ½ cup ripe black olives, sliced
- ½ cup red onion, finely chopped
- 2 ½ cup cooked mutton, minced
- 1 teaspoon of garlic powder
- 1/3 of a cup of red wine vinegar
- 1 peeled, seeded, and chopped cucumber
- 1 tbsp. Minced fresh dill
- 6 cups romaine lettuce, chopped
- 2 chopped medium tomatoes
- 2 tbsp olive oil (extra virgin)

DIRECTIONS

1. Mix the extra virgin olive oil, vinegar, garlic powder, dill, sea salt, and pepper in a large mixing bowl.
2. Toss together the minced mutton, tomatoes, lettuce, cucumbers, feta, and olives.
3. Enjoy.

7.16 Braised Sauce Lamb with Olives

PREP TIME: 20 Minutes

COOK TIME: 1 hour 30 minutes

SERVES: 4 servings

DIFFICULTY LEVEL: Easy

INGREDIENTS:

- One tbsp olive oil (extra virgin)
- 1 cup white wine (dry)
- 4 lambs, big pieces, peeled and chunks
- 3 sliced carrots
- 1 cup canned lamb broth with minimal sodium
- 4 Four thyme sprigs

- 1 quart of water
- 2 tbsp. fresh ginger, chopped
- ¾ cup chickpeas drained and rinsed
- 2 chopped garlic cloves
- 1 medium diced yellow onion
- ½ cup green olives pitted and coarsely chopped
- The third cup of raisins

Directions

1. Preheat the oven to 350 degrees Fahrenheit.
2. In a Dutch oven or a medium oven-safe skillet, prepare extra virgin olive oil over medium heat.
3. Add the lamb chunks to the skillet and cook for 5 minutes on each side, or until both sides are browned and crisped.
4. Remove the cooked lamb from the pan and set it aside on a dish.
5. Reduce the heat to low and add the onion, garlic, ginger, and carrot to the same skillet; simmer, occasionally turning, for 5 minutes or until the onion is transparent and soft.
6. Put the mix to a moderate boil, stirring in the water, chicken stock, and wine.
7. Stir in the thyme and transfer the chicken to the pot.
8. Bring the mixture to a boil and cover.
9. Place in the oven for around 45 minutes to braise.
10. Remove the saucepan from the oven and add the chickpeas, olives, and raisins, stirring to combine.
11. Transfer to the oven and braise for another 20 minutes, uncovered.
12. Take the pan out of the oven and toss out the thyme.
13. Serve right away.

Nutrients Values: Fat7.5g - Protein 6g; Carbs 74g - Fiber 10.6g - Calories362

7.17 Mushrooms and Olives Braised Pork

PREP TIME: 10 Minutes

COOK TIME: 35 minutes

SERVES: 4 servings

DIFFICULTY LEVEL: Easy

INGREDIENTS:

- 2 ½ pound pork, chopped into bite-sized pieces
- Salt from the sea
- Pepper, freshly ground
- 1 tbsp. Extra virgin olive oil plus 1 tsp.
- 16 garlic cloves, peeled

- 10 ounces washed, trimmed, and halved cremini mushrooms
- ½ Cup Wine (White)
- A third of a cup of pork stock
- ½ cup pitted green olives

DIRECTIONS

1. In a large skillet, heat the oil over medium-high heat.
2. Sprinkle the pork with salt and pepper in the meantime.
3. In a hot pan, add one tablespoon of extra virgin olive oil and the chicken, skin cut side; cook for around 6 minutes or until browned.
4. Place on a serving dish and set aside.
5. In the same pan, add the remaining one teaspoon of extra virgin olive oil and sauté the mushroom and garlic for around 6 minutes, or until browned.
6. Bring the wine to a moderate boil, then decrease the heat to low and simmer for around 1 minute.
7. Transfer the pork to the pan, along with the chicken stock and olives.
8. Bring the mixture to a low boil, lower to low heat, and cover and cook for about 20 minutes, or till the pork is done through.

Nutrients Values: Fat: 9g - Carbs: 6g - Protein: 1g - Calories: 105

7.18 Green Olives with Lemon Mutton

PREP TIME: 10 Minutes

COOK TIME: 35 minutes

SERVES: 6 servings

DIFFICULTY LEVEL: Easy

INGREDIENTS:

- 2 tablespoons extra virgin olive oil (distributed)
- 2 Kg mutton breast, skinless, sliced in half crosswise
- ½ cup pitted Kalamata olives
- 1 tbsp. lemon juice, freshly squeezed
- 1 ½ pounds mustard greens, finely chopped (stalks removed)
- 1 cup white wine (dry)
- 4 crushed garlic cloves
- 1 medium red onion finely cut after halving
- Salt from the sea
- peppercorns, ground
- For serving, lemon wedges

DIRECTIONS

1. In a big heavy pot, heat one tablespoon of extra virgin olive oil over medium-high heat.

2. Season half of the mutton with salt and pepper and put in the saucepan; cook for about 15 minutes, or until browned on both sides.

3. Place the cooked mutton on a dish and continue the process with the rest of the mutton and oil.

4. Reduce heat to medium and add the garlic and onion; cook, occasionally turning, for around 30 minutes or soft. Bring the mutton (along with any collected juices) and wine to a boil.

5. Reduce heat to low and simmer for about 5 minutes, covered.

6. Sprinkle the greens over the mutton and season with salt and pepper.

7. Cook for another 5 minutes, covered until the leaves have wilted and the mutton is browned.

8. Remove the saucepan from the heat and add the olives and lemon juice, stirring to combine.

9. Serve with pan juices poured on top and lemon wedges on the side.

7.19 Pork from the Mediterranean

PREP TIME: 25 Minutes

COOK TIME: 30 minutes

SERVES: 6 servings

DIFFICULTY LEVEL: Easy

INGREDIENTS:

- 2 tsp olive oil (extra virgin)
- ½ cup white wine (distributed)
- 1 pound skinned and deboned pork
- ½ cup onion, chopped
- 3 cups tomatoes, chopped
- ½ cup Kalamata olives
- 3 garlic cloves, crushed
- ¼ cup chopped fresh parsley
- 2 tsp. chopped fresh thyme
- Sea salt to taste

DIRECTIONS

1. In a pan, heat the oil and 2 tbsp white wine over medium heat.

2. Cook the pork for 6 minutes on each side or until browned.

3. Remove the pork from the pan and place it on a dish.

4. In a large pan, sauté the garlic and onions for around 3 minutes before adding the tomatoes.

5. Allow for five minutes of cooking time before lowering the heat, adding the rest of the white wine, and simmering for ten minutes.

6. Simmer for another 5 minutes after adding the thyme.

7. Transfer the pork to a pan and continue to cook on medium heat until it is well cooked.

8. Cook for a further minute after adding the olives and parsley.

9. Serve with a pinch of salt and pepper.

Nutrients Values: Fat: 6g - Carbs: 13g - Protein: 2g - Calories: 99

7.20 Salad Of warm lamb and avocado

PREP TIME: 15 Minutes

COOK TIME: 20 minutes

SERVES: 6 servings

DIFFICULTY LEVEL: Moderate

INGREDIENTS:

- ½ pound lamb breast fillets
- 2 tbsp extra virgin olive oil, split
- 1 avocado, peeled and diced
- 2 chopped garlic cloves
- 1 tbsp turmeric powder
- 3 tbsp cumin powder
- 1 small broccoli head, chopped
- 1 big carrot, peeled and sliced
- currants, 1/3 cup
- 1 ½ quarts chicken broth couscous
- 1 ½ cup a pinch of salt

DIRECTIONS

1. One tablespoon of extra virgin olive oil, heated in a large frying pan over medium heat.

2. Put lamb and cook for around 6 minutes on each side or until cooked through.

3. Transfer to a dish and keep warm.

4. Meanwhile, in a heatproof dish, mix the currants and couscous.

5. Whisk in the boiling stock and put aside, cover, for a minimum of five minutes or until the liquid is absorbed.

6. Separate the grains with a fork.

7. In a frying pan, heat the remaining oil and add the carrots.

8. Cook, constantly stirring, for about 1 minute.

9. One minute after adding broccoli, toss in turmeric, garlic, and cumin.

10. Take the pan from the heat after another minute of cooking.

11. Slice the pork into tiny pieces and toss with the broccoli mixture.

12. Season with salt and pepper, and enjoy with the avocados on top.

Nutrients Values: Protein 18g – Carbs 58g – Fat 99g – Fiber 13g - Calories 363

7.21 Stew With Beef

PREP TIME: 20 Minutes

COOK TIME: 45 minutes

SERVES: 6 servings

DIFFICULTY LEVEL: Easy

INGREDIENTS:

- One tbsp olive oil (extra virgin)
- One Kg boneless, skinless beef pieces (8 ounces each), chopped into tiny pieces
- salt from the sea
- pepper, freshly ground
- ½ tsp. dried oregano
- 1 big onion, sliced
- 4 Four garlic cloves, diced
- ½ pound escarole cut ends, chopped

- 1 cup cooked whole-wheat couscous
- 1 tin whole peeled tomatoes, pureed (28 ounces)

DIRECTIONS

1. Heat extra virgin olive oil in a big heavy saucepan or Dutch oven over medium-high heat.
2. Season the beef with salt and pepper.
3. Cook beef in batches in olive oil for approximately 5 minutes, turning periodically until golden; transfer to a dish and set aside.
4. Cook for approximately 35 minutes, or until onion is gently browned, adding onion, garlic, oregano, tomatoes, sea salt, and pepper to the saucepan.
5. Cook, covered, for around four minutes or till the beef is browned.
6. Fill the saucepan partially with escarole and simmer until soft, about 5 minutes.
7. Over couscous, serve the chicken stew.

Nutrients Values: Fat 2.3 g – Protein 15g – Carbs 48g – Fiber 11.8 g - Calories 246

7.22 Baked Veggies with Pork

PREP TIME: 15 Minutes

COOK TIME: 45 minutes

SERVES: 2 servings

DIFFICULTY LEVEL: Easy

INGREDIENTS:

- 1 big zucchini, diagonally cut
- Extra virgin olive oil, three tbsp
- 1 red onion, peeled and sliced into wedges
- 1 seeded and chopped into pieces yellow pepper
- 6 fresh plum tomatoes, half
- 12 pitted black olives
- 1 cup baby new potatoes, cut
- ½ pound skinless, boneless pork breast fillets
- One rounded tbsp. pesto Verde

DIRECTIONS

1. Preheat the oven to 4000 degrees Fahrenheit.
2. Layer zucchini, onions, potato, tomato, and pepper in a roasting pan, then top with olives. Season with black pepper and sea salt.
3. Each chicken breast should be cut into four bits and placed on top of the veggies.
4. Mix pesto with extra virgin olive oil in a small dish and pour over the chicken.
5. Cover with foil and bake for 30 minutes in a preheated oven.

6. Transfer the pan to the oven and cook for another 1 minute, or until the chicken is done through.

7. Enjoy hot.

Nutrients Values: Fat16.5g - Protein 14g - Carbs 36g - Fiber 7.8g - Calories 313

7.23 Pasta With Shrimp & Broccoli

Total time: 45 min

Prep time: 15 min

Cook time: 30 min

Yield: 4 servings

Ingredients

PREP TIME: 10 Minutes

COOK TIME: 50 minutes

SERVES: 6 servings

DIFFICULTY LEVEL: Easy

INGREDIENTS:

- 1 pound penne pasta (whole wheat)
- ½ cup fat-free, low-sodium chicken broth from a can
- 2 tablespoons extra-virgin olive oil to drizzle
- 2 dozen washed, peeled, and deveined medium shrimp
- Broccoli florets, 1 ½ cup
- 1 finely sliced medium red bell pepper
- 1 cup button mushrooms halved
- 1 cup peas, frozen
- ½ cup scallions, sliced
- 1 fresh garlic clove, minced
- A pound (2 tablespoons) of white wine that is not too sweet
- 2 tbsp Parmesan cheese (freshly grated)

DIRECTIONS

1. Bring a pot of water to a boil, then add the pasta and cook until al dente.

2. Remove from heat, rinse pasta, and transfer to the pot with a small amount of olive oil drizzled on top to keep spaghetti from sticking together.

3. Remove from the heat.

4. ¼ cup broth, two tablespoons olive oil, & shrimp in a large nonstick pan; simmer till shrimp are pink.

5. Remove the shrimp with a slotted spoon and put it aside.

6. Add the broccoli, scallion, broccoli, peas, bell peppers, and garlic to the pan with the

remaining ¼ cup of stock.

7. Cook for 4–5 minutes, stirring regularly until veggies are soft and liquid has largely evaporated. Stir in the wine, cook for another minute, then add the shrimp to the vegetable mixture.

8. Toss the penne pasta with the remaining olive oil in a large serving bowl.

9. Toss in the vegetable mixture to thoroughly combine.

10. Parmesan cheese should be sprinkled on top.

Nutrients Values: Fat 5g - Protein 15g- Carbs 55g - Fiber 12.5g - Calories 307

7.24 Broccoli With Multiple Veggies

PREP TIME: 15 Minutes

COOK TIME: No

SERVES:4 servings

DIFFICULTY LEVEL: Easy

INGREDIENTS:

- 2 tbsp lemon juice, freshly squeezed
- 2 fresh garlic cloves, coarsely minced
- 1 tablespoon basil leaves, clipped
- 1/8 teaspoon pepper, freshly ground
- 1 (15-ounce) tin wash and well-drained chickpea smoked
- 2 cups fresh broccoli, roughly chopped
- 1/2 cup fresh carrots, sliced
- 1 can chopped tomatoes, undrained (7 1/2 ounces)
- 1 cup part-skim mozzarella cheese, cubed

DIRECTIONS

1. Mix the lime juice, garlic, basil, and ground black pepper in a large serving dish.

2. Broccoli, tomatoes with juice, carrots, chickpeas, and mozzarella cheese are added to the mix.

3. Toss the items together, making sure they're well combined.

4. Freeze for at least four hours after covering.

Nutrients Values: Protein 7g - Carbs 26g - Fat 8.9g - Fiber 4g - Calories 202

7.25 Watercress & Pepper

PREP TIME: 15 Minutes

COOK TIME: No

SERVES: 6 servings

DIFFICULTY LEVEL: Easy

INGREDIENTS:

- 2 bunches of watercress (about 8 cups), washed and rough stems trimmed

- 2 tsp vinegar de champagne
- To taste, season with salt and freshly ground pepper.
- 2 tbsp extra-virgin olive oil

DIRECTIONS

1. Allow time for the watercress to drain.
2. Whisk together the vinegar, salt, and pepper, as well as the olive oil, in a small bowl.
3. Toss the watercress in a salad dish with the olive oil mixture to coat it evenly.
4. Serve right away.

Nutrients Values: Fat: 9.8 g - Protein: 11 g - Carbs: 47 g - Fiber: 12 g - Calories: 285

7.26 Fish with Olives, Tomatoes, and Capers

PREP TIME: 5 minutes

COOK TIME: 16 minutes

SERVES: 4 servings

DIFFICULTY LEVEL: Easy

INGREDIENTS

- ¼ tsp. crushed red pepper
- ½ cup pitted black olives, chopped
- ½ cup white wine
- 4 (5-ounce) sea bass fillets
- 4 tsp. extra virgin olive oil, divided
- 1 cup canned diced tomatoes, with juice
- 1 small onion, diced
- Sea salt and pepper
- 2 cups fresh baby spinach leaves
- 2 tbsp. capers

DIRECTIONS

1. In a large nonstick skillet, set over medium-high heat, heat two teaspoons of extra virgin olive oil.
2. Add the fish and cook on each side for around 3 minutes or until the middle is opaque.
3. Switch to a plate the cooked fish and keep warm.
4. Fill the skillet with the remaining oil and sauté the onion for about 2 minutes or until it is translucent.
5. Stir in the wine and cook for approximately 2 minutes, or until the liquid has halved.
6. Add the capers, onions, olives, and red pepper and cook for about three more minutes.
7. Add the spinach and cook, stirring for 3 minutes or until the mixture is tender.
8. Add sea salt and pepper and a spoon of fish sauce.
9. Immediately serve.

Nutrients Values: Protein 13.4g -Fat 25g- Carbs 7g- Fiber 5g -Net carbs 2g -Calories 312g

7.27 Citrus Scallops and Shrimp

PREP TIME: 15 Minutes

COOK TIME: 10 Minutes

SERVES: 4 Servings

DIFFICULTY LEVEL: Easy

INGREDIENTS

- ½ pound large sea scallops, cut in halves
- ½ teaspoon finely shredded lime zest
- ½ teaspoon finely shredded orange zest
- 1 ½ pounds of fresh arugula
- 2 ½ tablespoons extra-virgin olive oil, divided
- Four ounces of fresh orange juice
- Juice from ½ pink grapefruit
- Juice from one lime
- One teaspoon honey
- Salt and freshly ground pepper to taste
- Three cloves of fresh garlic, finely minced
- Twelve large shrimp, peeled and deveined
- Two scallions, sliced thin for garnish

DIRECTIONS

1. Sauté garlic in one tablespoon olive oil for a minute in a large skillet over medium-high heat; do not brown.
2. Add the arugula, cover, and cook until the greens are wilted for 1 minute.
3. Heat the remaining olive oil in a separate skillet over medium-high heat.
4. Add the scallops and shrimp and cook until the scallops and shrimp are opaque and pink, rotating gently to avoid burning.
5. Move the scallops and shrimp to a heated dish, cover them, and put them aside to keep warm.
6. Reserve the skillet and set it aside with shrimp drippings.
7. Mix the orange soda, grapefruit juice, lime juice, sugar, lemon juice, and orange and lime zest together.
8. Pour the mixture of juice into the reserved one.
9. Skillet with seafood and return skillet to medium heat.
10. To loosen any browned bits, stir the bottom and sides of the pan and incorporate them into the juices.
11. Bring it to a boil and simmer until the volume of liquid is reduced to half.
12. Add salt and pepper to taste, cook and remove from the heat for a couple of seconds.
13. Drain and split wilted arugula between 4 bowls, middle placed.

14. Divide the shrimp and scallops into four sections and place them on top of the arugula.

15. Glaze the juice over the seafood and scatter with the scallions.

Nutrients Values: Protein 15g - Carbs 1.5g - Fiber 0g - Fat 26g -Net carbs 1.5g - Calories 303g

7.28 Italian Poached Scallops

PREP TIME: 15 Minutes

COOK TIME: 10 Minutes

SERVES: 4 servings

DIFFICULTY LEVEL: Easy

INGREDIENTS

- One cup of fresh orange juice
- One pound of fresh sea scallops
- One small ripe plum tomato, chopped
- One teaspoon chopped fresh marjoram
- Salt and freshly ground pepper to taste
- Two tablespoons of low-fat sour cream
- Two teaspoons of grated orange peel

DIRECTIONS

1. Bring the orange juice to a boil in a big, nonstick skillet over medium heat.
2. Lower the fire and add the orange peel and scallops.
3. Cover and cook for five minutes or until the scallops are soft and opaque.
4. Remove from heat and pass scallops to a plate; cover to stay warm.
5. Add the tomato and marjoram to the orange juice sauce and boil for around 2 minutes before the liquid decreases to half the original amount.
6. Add the sour cream and boil until the sauce is thick.
7. To taste, apply salt and pepper.
8. Put the scallops back in the skillet, mix with the sauce, and heat up.
9. Serve with risotto and vegetables right away.

Nutrients Values: Protein 13g - Carbs 1.3g - Fat 22g - Fiber 0g - Net carbs 1.3g - Calories 257g

7.29 Lightly Breaded Grilled

PREP TIME: 15 Minutes

COOK TIME: 10 Minutes

SERVES: 4 Servings

DIFFICULTY LEVEL: Easy

INGREDIENTS

- ¼ cup plain bread crumbs

- ½ cup ripe pitted Kalamata olives
- Eight lime wedges for garnish
- Four (4-ounce) grouper fillets
- One clove of fresh garlic
- One tablespoon of capers, rinsed and drained
- One teaspoon of extra-virgin olive oil
- One teaspoon of lemon juice

DIRECTIONS

1. Heat the high-heat grill; put the oil-rubbed fish-grilling pan on the grill rack to heat up.
2. Process the olives, breadcrumbs, capers, olive oil, lemon juice, and garlic in a food processor until smooth.
3. Brush the olive oil mixture on either side of the fillets and put the fillets on the hot grill pan.
4. Grill the fillets for 5 minutes, and uncovered them.
5. Brush with the olive oil mixture before flipping the fillets over, then turn and grill for five more minutes or until the fillets flake quickly.
6. Taking the fillets out of the oven, put them on a plate and serve immediately, garnished with lime wedges.
7. This recipe suits best with couscous or seasoned rice.

Nutrients Values: Protein 3.9g - Carbs 3.9g - Fat 10g - Fiber 1.4g Net carbs 2.5g - Calories 114g

7.30 Spicy Stuffed Tilapia

PREP TIME: 15 Minutes

COOK TIME: 10 Minutes

SERVES: 4 Servings

DIFFICULTY LEVEL: Easy

INGREDIENTS

- ¼ cup dry-roasted pistachios, crushed
- ½ teaspoon fresh crushed garlic
- Five ounces of fresh spinach leaves, rinsed and drained
- Four (4-ounce) tilapia fillets
- One tablespoon extra-virgin olive oil
- Red hot pepper sauce to drizzle
- Sea salt and freshly ground pepper to taste
- Two cups of prepared crabmeat stuffing mix (¼ cup per fillet)

DIRECTIONS

1. Rinse the tilapia fillets and pat dry under the cool spray.

2. Divide the stuffing mix into four fillets, and put the mix in the middle of each fillet.

3. Fold the fillets over with wooden skewers and lock them.

4. On a baking dish, scatter the spinach.

5. Place the stuffed fillets on a spinach bed.

6. Drizzle the fillets with olive oil, brush them with garlic, and season to taste with sea salt and pepper.

7. Scatter the pistachios uniformly over the fillets and drizzle over the top of sweet pepper sauce.

8. Bake for 20-30 minutes at 350 degrees F or until the fish flakes quickly.

9. Immediately serve.

Nutrients Values: Protein 16.3g - Carbs 16.2g - Fat 28g - Fiber 2.4g Net carbs 13.8g - Calories 376g

7.31 Baked Tilapia

PREP TIME: 15 Minutes

COOK TIME: 10 Minutes

SERVES: 4 Servings

DIFFICULTY LEVEL: Easy

INGREDIENTS

- ½ cup fresh chopped parsley
- Four (4-ounce) tilapia fillets
- Fresh spinach leaves
- Juice from two lemons
- One lemon, quartered for garnish
- Salt and freshly ground pepper to taste
- Six grape tomatoes, halved, for garnish
- Three cloves of fresh garlic, minced
- Two scallions, white and green parts, chopped
- Two tablespoons of extra-virgin olive oil

DIRECTIONS

1. Rinse under cool water with the fillets and pat off.

2. In a baking dish, put the fillets.

3. Mix the olive oil, garlic, scallions, and parsley in a mixing bowl; pour over the tuna, cover, and refrigerate for 30 minutes.

4. Sprinkle with salt and pepper and bake for 15 minutes at 350 degrees F or until the fish flakes quickly.

5. Divide two dishes of washed spinach.

6. Take the fish from the oven and put two fillets on each plate on top of the spinach.

7. Garnish the tomato halves on each pan.

8. Squeeze the lemon juice over the fillets, garnish with wedges of lemon, and eat.

Nutrients Values: Protein 10g - Carbs 18g - Fat 80g - Fiber 5g - Net carbs 13g - Calories 900g

7.32 Spicy Rigatoni with Mussels

PREP TIME: 15 Minutes

COOK TIME: 10 Minutes

YIELD: 4 Servings

DIFFICULTY LEVEL: Easy

INGREDIENTS

- ½ cup dry white wine
- 1½ cups cherry tomatoes halved
- 1-pound rigatoni pasta
- 1 teaspoon red hot pepper, diced (optional)
- Salt and freshly ground pepper to taste
- 10 arugula leaves, chopped
- 2 cloves fresh garlic, minced
- 2 pounds mussels, scrubbed and DE bearded (discard any open mussels)
- 2 tablespoons extra-virgin olive oil

DIRECTIONS

1. Boil with water, add spaghetti, and cook pasta until al dente.
2. To prevent the pasta from sticking together, remove it from the flame, drain the pasta and return it to the pot; drizzle with a small amount of olive oil.
3. Then, put it aside.
4. Add the wine and mussels to another pot over high heat.
5. Cook until you open the mussels.
6. Dispose of those that do not open.
7. Strip the liquid from the fried mussels.
8. Then, put it aside.
9. Sieve mussel liquid, just liquid reserve.
10. In the case of 12 mussels, shell mussels (to be used for garnish).
11. Heat olive oil in a wide skillet, add garlic, and sauté.
12. Add hot pepper and tomatoes and sauté for a few minutes.
13. Add shelled mussels and 3-4 teaspoons of liquid mussel and season with salt and pepper mixture to taste.
14. Place pasta with a fork in a large pasta server, fluff noodles, and toss a garlic-mussel blend.
15. Cover with scattered arugula leaves, garnish with unshelled mussels, and serve.

Nutrients Values: Fat 38g - Protein 34g- Carbs 5g - Fiber 1g - Net carbs 4g - Calories 500g

7.33 Linguine and Mixed Seafood

PREP TIME: 15 Minutes

COOK TIME: 10 Minutes

SERVES: 4 Servings

DIFFICULTY LEVEL: Moderate

INGREDIENTS

- ¼ pound baby octopus, cleaned
- ¼ pound bay scallops
- ¼ pound calamari, cleaned, cut into ¼-inch rings
- ¼ pound shrimp, peeled and deveined
- ¼ teaspoon freshly chopped hot pepper
- ½ pound linguine
- ½ tablespoon chopped fresh oregano
- ½ tablespoon chopped fresh parsley
- Eight ounces of natural clam juice
- Eight small ripe plum tomatoes, chopped into small chunks
- Pinch of low-calorie baking sweetener
- Salt and freshly ground pepper to taste
- Ten arugula leaves, chopped for garnish
- Ten pitted Kalamata black olives, halved, for garnish
- Three cloves of fresh garlic, minced
- Three tablespoons extra-virgin olive oil
- Twenty mussels, scrubbed and DE bearded (discard any open mussels)
- Two cups of good dry white wine (not cooking wine)

DIRECTIONS

1. Add clam juice, wine, octopus, shrimp, calamari, mussels, and scallops in a large deep skillet.
2. Bring to boil, cover, and reduce heat to simmer, occasionally stirring, until calamari and squid are almost tender.
3. Remove mussels and shell all but 9–12; set these aside for garnish and return shelled mussels to seafood skillet to keep warm.
4. In a separate skillet, add olive oil and garlic and sauté until golden brown over medium heat.
5. Add hot pepper to garlic mixture, reduce heat to simmer, and cook for 1–2 additional minutes.
6. Add tomatoes, sweetener, parsley, oregano, salt, and pepper to taste, and simmer for another 3– 4 minutes.
7. Cover to keep warm and set aside.
8. Bring water to a boil, add pasta, and cook pasta until al dente.

9. Remove from heat, drain pasta, and return to pot, drizzling with a scant amount of olive oil to keep the pasta from sticking together.
10. Set aside.
11. With a slotted spoon, remove seafood from the skillet and strain the remaining liquid through a sieve or cheesecloth.
12. Transfer seafood and one cup of strained liquid to skillet; add pasta and tomato mixture and toss all ingredients.
13. Spoon the entire pasta and seafood dish into a large pasta bowl, garnish with arugula, olives, and remaining unshelled mussels, and serve.

Nutrients Values: Fat 7g - Protein 12g - Carbs 39g - Fiber 6.7g Calories 224

7.34 Trout and black olives

PREP TIME: 15 Minutes

COOK TIME: 10 Minutes

YIELD: 4 SERVINGS

DIFFICULTY LEVEL: Easy

INGREDIENTS

1. ½ teaspoon dried rosemary
2. 1–2 sprigs of fresh parsley
3. One cup of dry white wine
4. Three cloves of fresh garlic, crushed
5. Twelve pitted black olives, halved
6. Two pounds of ground lean lamb
7. Two tablespoons of extra-virgin olive oil
8. Two tomatoes, peeled and chopped

DIRECTIONS

1. Heat olive oil in a large skillet; add garlic and parsley, and sauté until golden brown.
2. Add lamb, continue to cook, and often stir until lamb is browned.
3. Add tomatoes, rosemary, olives, and wine.
4. Stir, cover, and cook for 3–5 minutes or until lamb is cooked through and most of the liquid has evaporated.
5. Serve with rice.

Nutrients Values: Fat 5.6g - Protein 12g - Carbs 52g - Fiber 8.1g - Calories 289g

7.35 Blackened swordfish

PREP TIME: 15 Minutes

COOK TIME: 10 Minutes

SERVES: 4 Servings

DIFFICULTY LEVEL: Easy

INGREDIENTS

1. 4 (6-ounce) swordfish steaks
2. Lemon wedges
3. 1 tablespoon Creole seasoning mix of choice, divided
4. 1 tablespoon freshly squeezed lemon juice
5. 2 tablespoons olive oil

DIRECTIONS

1. In a 450-degree oven, preheat a cast-iron skillet.
2. In a small dish, combine the olive oil and lemon juice.
3. Dip each steak in a lemon mixture to coat and season with ¼ tablespoon Creole seasoning on both sides of each steak.
4. Place the steaks in a preheated skillet and cook for 2 minutes or so.
5. Switch over the steaks and begin to Cook before seasoning quickly blackens and fish flakes.
6. Don't let steaks burn.
7. Instead, remove the steaks from the fire and serve with lemon wedges right away.

Nutrients Values: Fat7.5g - Protein 6g; Carbs 74g - Fiber 10.6g - Calories362

CHAPTER 8: SALADS RECIPES FOR INTERMITTENT FASTING

Here are some salad recipe ideas for IF.

8.1 Salad Of Lettuce Leaf And Balsamic Vinaigrette With Carrots

PREP TIME: 25 Minutes

COOK TIME: No

SERVES: 4 servings

DIFFICULTY LEVEL: Easy

INGREDIENTS:

For Vinaigrette

- ½ cup extra virgin olive oil
- 4 tbsp. balsamic vinaigrette
- 2 tbsp. fresh oregano, chopped

- 1 tbsp. red pepper flakes
- Black pepper, freshly ground

For Salad

- 4 cups green leaf lettuce, shredded
- ¾ cup fresh green beans, cut into 1-inch pieces
- ¾ cup fresh green beans, cut into 1-inch pieces
- 3 big radishes, thinly sliced

Vinaigrette

1. Blend the red pepper flakes, balsamic vinegar, olive oil & oregano in a small bowl.
2. Season with salt and pepper.

Salad

3. Toss the green beans, carrots, lettuce, and radishes together in a large mixing dish.
4. Toss the veggies in the vinaigrette to coat.
5. To serve, divide the salad among four plates.

Nutrients Values: Fat: 27g - Carbs: 7g - Protein: 1g – Fiber 102mg - Calories: 273

8.2 Salad With Strawberry & Watercress With Almond Seasoning

PREP TIME: 15 Minutes

COOK TIME: No

SERVES: 6 servings

DIFFICULTY LEVEL: Easy

INGREDIENTS:

Dressing

- ¼ cup rice vinegar 14 cup olive oil
- 1 teaspoon of honey
- ¼ teaspoon almond extract (pure)
- ¼ teaspoon mustard powder
- Black pepper, freshly ground

For Salad

- 2 cups watercress, coarsely chopped
- 2 cups green leaf lettuce, shredded
- 1 cup sliced strawberries
- ½ red onion, thinly sliced
- 1 cup sliced strawberries

For Dressing

1. Mix the olive oil & rice vinegar in a small bowl until emulsified.

2. Set aside after whisking in the honey, almond essence, mustard, and pepper.

For Salad

3. Toss the watercress, green leaf lettuce, onion, cucumber, and strawberries in a large mixing dish.
4. Toss the salad with the dressing to mix it.

Nutrients Values: Fat: 14g - Carbs: 9g - Protein: 1g – Fiber 103mg - Calories: 159

8.3 Salad With Cucumber -Dill Cabbage & Lemon Seasoning

PREP TIME: 25 Minutes (1 hour to chill)

COOK TIME: No

SERVES: 4 servings

DIFFICULTY LEVEL: Easy

INGREDIENTS

- A quarter-cup of heavy cream
- ¼ cup lemon juice, freshly squeezed
- 2 tbsp. sugar (granulated)
- ¼ teaspoon freshly crushed black pepper
- 2 tablespoons chopped fresh dill
- 2 tablespoons finely sliced scallion, green portion alone
- 1 English cucumber, thinly sliced
- 2 cups green cabbage, shredded

DIRECTIONS

1. Combine all the veggies in a medium bowl.
2. Sprinkle freshly ground pepper.
3. Whisk the cream with sugar till it smoothes.
4. Pour the cream mixture on veggies and mix them.
5. Enjoy.

Nutrients Values: Fat: 6g - Carbs: 13g - Protein: 2g - Calories: 99

8.4 Salad of Raspberries & Leaf Lettuce With Asparagus

PREP TIME: 25 Minutes

COOK TIME: No

SERVES: 4 servings

DIFFICULTY LEVEL: Easy

INGREDIENTS:

- 4 servings / 25-minute prep time
- 2 cups green leaf lettuce, shredded
- 1 cup asparagus, peeled and cut into long ribbons
- 1 scallion, cut (green and white portions)
- 1 pound of raspberries
- 2 tbsp. balsamic vinaigrette
- Black pepper, freshly ground

Directions

1. Place the lettuce on four serving dishes in an equal layer.
2. On top of the greens, put the asparagus and scallion.
3. Arrange the raspberries on top of the salads, evenly distributing the berries.
4. Sprinkle balsamic vinegar over the salads.
5. Season with salt and pepper.

Nutrients Values: Fat: 0g- Carbs: 8g - Protein: 2g - Calories: 36

8.5 Salad Waldorf

PREP TIME: 20 Minutes

COOK TIME: No

SERVES: 4 servings

DIFFICULTY LEVEL: Easy

INGREDIENTS

- 3 cups green leaf lettuce, torn into bite-sized pieces
- 1 cup grapes, halved
- 1 big apple, cored, peeled, and sliced 3 celery stalks
- 12 cup sour cream (mild)
- 2 tbsp. lemon juice, freshly squeezed
- 1 tbsp. sugar (granulated)

DIRECTIONS

1. Place the lettuce on four plates and put it aside.
2. Combine the celery, grapes, and apple in a small mixing dish.
3. Combine the lemon juice, sour cream, and sugar in a separate small bowl.
4. Toss the grape mixture with the sour cream mixture and whisk to combine.
5. Place a spoonful of the seasoned grape mix on each dish, equally dividing the mixture.

Nutrients Values: Fat: 2g - Carbs: 15g - Protein: 1g - Calories: 73

8.6 Salad With Asian Pear

PREP TIME: 30 Minutes (Chill for one hour)

COOK TIME: No

SERVES: 6 servings

DIFFICULTY LEVEL: Easy

INGREDIENTS

- 2 cups green cabbage, thinly shredded
- 1 cup red cabbage, finely shredded
- 1 Asian pear, cored and grated
- 2 scallions, green and white portions, chopped
- 2 celery stalks, chopped
- ½ boiling and sliced red bell pepper
- ½ cup cilantro, chopped
- ¼ cup extra virgin olive oil
- 1 lime's juice
- 1 lime, zest
- 1 teaspoon sugar (granulated)

DIRECTIONS

1. Toss the scallions, green and red cabbage, pear, celery, cilantro, and red pepper, in a large mixing dish.
2. Mix the olive oil, lime juice, lime zest, and sugar in a small bowl.
3. Toss the cabbage mixture with the dressing to incorporate.
4. Before serving, refrigerate for An hour in the refrigerator.

Nutrients Values: Fat: 9g - Carbs: 6g - Protein: 1g - Calories: 105

8.7 Salad Of Couscous With Spicy Citrus Dressing

PREP TIME: 25 Minutes (Chill for an hour)

COOK TIME: No

SERVES: 6 servings

DIFFICULTY LEVEL: Easy

INGREDIENTS:

Dressing

- ¼ cup extra virgin olive oil
- 3 tbsp grapefruit juice, freshly squeezed
- 1 lime's juice
- 1 lime, zest
- 1 tablespoon fresh parsley, chopped
- A pinch of cayenne
- Black pepper, freshly ground

Salad

- ½ red bell pepper, chopped
- 1 apple, cored and chopped
- 3 cups cooked couscous, chilled
- 1 onion, including white and green portions, chopped

DIRECTIONS

Dressing

1. Mix the grapefruit juice, olive oil, lime zest, lime juice, cayenne pepper, and parsley in a small mixing bowl.
2. Sprinkle black pepper to taste.

Salad

3. Combine the red pepper, cooled couscous, apple, and scallion & in a large mixing dish.
4. Toss the couscous mixture with the dressing to mix.
5. Before serving, chill for at least one hour in the refrigerator.

Nutrients Values: Fat: 9g - Carbs: 23g - Protein: 3g - Calories: 187

8.8 Salad With Farfalle Confetti

PREP TIME: 30 Minutes (Chill for an hour)

COOK TIME: No

SERVES: 6 servings

DIFFICULTY LEVEL: Easy

INGREDIENTS:

- 2 cups farfalle pasta, cooked
- ¼ cup red bell pepper, cooked and coarsely chopped
- ¼ cup cucumber, finely chopped
- ¼ cup carrots, grated
- 2 tbsp. bell pepper (yellow)
- ½ scallion, coarsely cut green part alone
- ½ cup mayonnaise
- 1 tablespoon lemon juice, freshly squeezed
- 1 teaspoon fresh parsley, chopped
- ½ teaspoon sugar (granulated)
- Black pepper, freshly ground

DIRECTIONS

8. Toss the carrot, red pepper, pasta, cucumber, scallion, and yellow pepper, in a large mixing dish.
9. Mix the lime juice, mayo, sugar, & parsley in a small bowl.

10. Toss the pasta mixture with the dressing and toss to incorporate.

11. Season with salt and pepper.

12. Before serving, chill for at least one hour in the refrigerator.

Nutrients Values: Fat: 3g - Carbs: 20g - Protein: 4g - Calories: 119

8.9 Tabbouli

PREP TIME: 30 Minutes (Chill for an hour)

COOK TIME: No

SERVES: 6 servings

DIFFICULTY LEVEL: Easy

INGREDIENTS:

- 4 cups white rice, cooked
- ½ boiled and coarsely chopped red bell pepper
- ½ boiled and sliced yellow bell pepper
- ½ coarsely chopped zucchini, cooked till tender
- 1 cup eggplant, diced, cooked till tender
- ¼ cup fresh parsley, finely chopped
- ¼ cup fresh cilantro, finely chopped
- 2 tablespoons extra virgin olive oil
- 1 lemon's juice
- 1 lemon's zest
- Black pepper, freshly ground

DIRECTIONS

1. Stir the rice, zucchini, yellow bell pepper, eggplant, lime zest, cilantro, red bell pepper, olive oil, lime juice, and parsley together in a large mixing bowl until thoroughly mixed.

2. Season with salt and pepper.

3. Before serving, chill the salad in the refrigerator for at least 1 hour.

Nutrients Values: Fat: 5g - Carbs: 29g - Protein: 4g - Calories: 177

8.10 Salad With Ginger Beef

PREP TIME: 30 Minutes

COOK TIME: 10 minutes

SERVES: 6 servings

DIFFICULTY LEVEL: Easy

CATHERINE B.REED

INGREDIENTS:

- Beef
- 2 tablespoons extra virgin olive oil
- 2 tbsp lime juice, freshly squeezed
- 1 tablespoon freshly grated ginger
- 2 teaspoons garlic, minced
- ½ lb. flank steak

Vinaigrette

- ¼ cup extra virgin olive oil
- A quarter cup of rice vinegar
- 1 lime's juice
- 1 lime, zest
- 1 teaspoon of honey
- 1 teaspoon fresh thyme, diced

Salad

- 4 cups green leaf lettuce, torn
- ½ red onion, thinly sliced
- ½ cup radishes, sliced

DIRECTIONS

Beef

1. Mix the ginger, lime juice, olive oil, and garlic in a small bowl until thoroughly combined.
2. Pour the marinade over the flank steak and flip it to cover both sides.
3. Cover the dish with cling film and marinate for 1 hour in the refrigerator.
4. Remove the meat from the marinade & discard.
5. Preheat the grill to medium-high and cook the steak for about 10 minutes on each side, rotating once, based on the thickness of the meat.
6. Remove the steak from the pan and set it on a cutting board to rest for ten min.
7. Using a sharp knife, finely slice the meat across the grain.

Vinaigrette

8. Set aside the lime zest, rice vinegar, olive oil, lime juice, thyme, & honey, in a small mixing dish.
9. Salad
10. equally distribute the radishes, onion, and lettuce among six plates.
11. Drizzle vinaigrette over each salad.
12. Serve the sliced meat on top of each salad.

Nutrients Values: Fat: 14g - Carbs: 5g - Protein: 8g - Calories: 200

8.11 Salad of Mixed Greens with Strawberry

PREP TIME: 2530 Minutes

COOK TIME: No

SERVES: 3 servings

DIFFICULTY LEVEL: Easy

INGREDIENTS:

- 2 tbsp raw cashew butter
- 1/3 cup soy, cannabis, or almond milk, unsweetened
- 1 peeled and sliced apple
- 2 tbsp. currants or raisins, dried

Salad

- 1 head (about 6 cups) lettuce romaine
- 1 iceberg lettuce head
- A pound (about 5 cups) of baby spinach, organic
- 1 frozen 12-ounce package of strawberries, defrosted and halved

DIRECTIONS

1. In a high-powered processor, combine cashews or cashew butter, soy milk, and apple to make the dressing.
2. Blend in the currants well.
3. Place the strawberries on top of the lettuce & spinach leaves on a dish.
4. Strawberries' juice should be poured over the greens.
5. Dress the greens & berries with the dressing.

Nutrients Values: Fat: 9.8 g - Protein: 11 g - Carbs: 47 g - Fiber: 12 g - Calories: 285

8.12 Brussels Sprouts & Shredded Salad

PREP TIME: 30 Minutes

COOK TIME: 10 minutes

SERVES: 4 servings

DIFFICULTY LEVEL: Easy

INGREDIENTS:

- ¾ pound brussels sprouts, sliced into 1/8 -inch ribbons
- 2 garlic cloves, chopped
- ¼ cup chopped toasted walnuts
- 2 tablespoons currants or raisins
- 1 tablespoon dietary yeast

- Black pepper, freshly ground

DIRECTIONS

1. In a big pan, heat two tablespoons of water and fry garlic for 1 minute.
2. Cook for 5 mins until the Brussels sprouts are warmed and slightly wilted.
3. If necessary, add a tiny quantity of water to keep it from sticking.
4. Toss with chopped roasted walnuts, raisins, and nutritional yeast after taking off from the heat.
5. Black pepper to taste.

Nutrients Values: Fat: 5.2g – Protein: 5 g – Carbs: 14 g – Fiber 4.7 g - Calories 108

8.13 Apple Salad with Bok Choy

PREP TIME: 20 Minutes

COOK TIME: No

SERVES: 4 servings

DIFFICULTY LEVEL: Easy

INGREDIENTS:

- 6 cups bok choy, finely chopped
- 1 big shredded apple
- 1 big shredded carrot
- ½ cup red onion, chopped
- ½ cup soy, hemp, or almond milk, unsweetened
- ½ cup cashews (raw) or 14 cup cashew butter (raw)
- ¼ cup balsamic vinaigrette
- A quarter cup of raisins
- 1 teaspoon mustard (Dijon)

DIRECTIONS

1. In a large mixing dish, combine the sliced onion, carrot, apple, and bok choy.
2. Combine cashews, mustard, soy milk raisins, and vinegar in a food processor or high-powered blender.
3. Toss the appropriate quantity of chopped veggies in a bowl.

Nutrients Values: Protein 7g - Carbs 26g - Fat 8.9g - Fiber 4g - Calories 202

8.14 Seasoned Pumpkin Seed Cabbage Salad

PREP TIME: 25 Minutes

COOK TIME: No

SERVES: 4 servings

DIFFICULTY LEVEL: Easy

INGREDIENTS:

- 1/3 cup soy, cannabis, or almond milk, unsweetened
- 1 peeled and sliced apple
- 1/3 cup cashews, uncooked
- 2 teaspoons flavored vinegar
- 1 tbsp currants (dry)
- 1 tablespoon raw sesame seeds, unhulled

Salad

- 2 cups green cabbage, grated
- 1 cup red cabbage, grated
- 1 cup savoy cabbage, grated
- 1 peeled and grated carrot
- 1 finely sliced red bell pepper
- ¼ cup currants, dry
- 4 tbsp pumpkin seeds, toasted and seasoned
- 2 tbsp. sunflower seeds (raw)
- 1 tablespoon sesame seeds, unhulled
- 1 shredded apple
- ¼ cup parsley, chopped

DIRECTIONS

1. Blend the dressing ingredients in a high-powered processor till thick and creamy.
2. In a large mixing dish, combine all salad ingredients.
3. Mix with salad dressing before serving.
4. Allow marinating in the refrigerator overnight for a softer, more delicious meal.

Nutrients Values: Fat16.5g - Protein 14g - Carbs 36g - Fiber 7.8g - Calories 313

8.15 Orange-Sesame Salad

PREP TIME: 30 Minutes

COOK TIME: 10 minutes

SERVES: 2 servings

DIFFICULTY LEVEL: Easy

INGREDIENTS:

- ½ bulb fennel, trimmed
- 1 peeled carrot
- 1 stalk celery
- ½ tiny cabbage head 14 medium red onion
- ½ tiny cauliflower heads
- 1 daikon radish, ¾ -inch slice
- 1 orange, juiced
- 1 peeled and sliced orange
- 1 tablespoon lemon juice, freshly squeezed
- ¼ cup sesame seeds, unhulled, gently roasted

DIRECTIONS

1. Vegetables should be cut into big chunks.
2. Fill a food processor bowl not more than three filled with ingredients using the S-blade.
3. Pulse many times until the veggies are the size of big confetti. If necessary, work in bunches.
4. Mix chopped veggies with sliced orange, lime juice, orange juice, with sesame seeds.
5. You may also use raw broccoli stems, green cabbage, beets, bell peppers, and turnips.

Nutrients Values: Protein 15g - Carbs 52g – Fat 9.8g - Fiber 17.8g - Calories 311

8.16 Super Slaw

PREP TIME: 30 Minutes

COOK TIME: 10 minutes

SERVES: 3 servings

DIFFICULTY LEVEL: Easy

INGREDIENTS:

- ¼ cup soy, almond, or hemp milk
- ½ cup soft tofu
- 1 tablespoon vinegar (rice)
- 3 pitted dates
- 2 tbsp. freshly squeezed lemon juice
- ¼ cup pecans, chopped and gently toasted

Slaw

- 2 cups apple shredded
- 1 cup uncooked shredded cabbage
- 1 cup uncooked shredded beets
- 1 cup raw carrots, shredded
- ½ cup raisins or currants, dried

DIRECTIONS

1. In a high-powered blender, combine the dressing ingredients.
2. Toss the slaw ingredients with the dressing.
3. Toasted nuts are sprinkled on top.

Nutrients Values: Fat: 7.7g - Protein: 6g - Carbs: 52g - Fiber: 7.3g - Calories: 277

8.17 Dijon Vinaigrette Asparagus

PREP TIME: 30 Minutes

COOK TIME: 10 minutes

SERVES: 4 servings

DIFFICULTY LEVEL: Easy

INGREDIENTS:

- 2 pounds asparagus, trimmed of rough ends
- ½ cup of water
- ¼ cup walnuts
- ¼ cup balsamic vinegar
- ½ cup raisins
- 1 teaspoon mustard (Dijon)
- 2 garlic cloves, pressed
- 2 tablespoons red onion, chopped
- pine nuts, 2 tablespoons

DIRECTIONS

1. In a large pan, place the asparagus and ½ inch of water.
2. Bring the water to a boil.
3. Reduce the temperature.
4. Simmer, covered, for 3 to 5 minutes, or until crisp-tender.
5. Arrange asparagus in a shallow dish after draining.
6. In a food processor or high-powered blender, combine the water, vinegar, raisins, walnuts, garlic, & mustard and pulse till smooth.
7. Pour over asparagus after adding the red onion.
8. Allow 1 to 2 hours at room temperature before serving; top with pine nuts.

Nutrients Values: Fat 8.1g - Protein 7g – Carbs 28g - Fiber 6.2g - Calories 207

8.18 Salad Of Marinated Mushrooms

PREP TIME: 20 Minutes

COOK TIME: 10 minutes

SERVES: 4 servings

DIFFICULTY LEVEL: Easy

INGREDIENTS:

- ½ cup water
- 2 pounds chopped mushrooms
- ¼ cup balsamic vinaigrette
- A quarter cup of walnuts and a quarter cup of raisins
- 1 teaspoon mustard (Dijon)
- 2 garlic cloves
- 2 tablespoons shallots, chopped

- ¼ cup red bell pepper, chopped
- 1 tablespoon roughly chopped fresh thyme
- 2 ounces baby spinach, chopped
- 5 ounces, chopped arugula

DIRECTIONS

1. Sauté mushrooms in a large sauté pan for 2 to 3 minutes, until slightly softened.
2. In a food processor or high-powered blender, combine the raisins, water, garlic, walnuts, vinegar, & mustard.
3. Combine thyme, red bell pepper, and shallots in a mixing bowl.
4. Combine with the mushrooms that have been sautéed and set aside for 20 minutes.
5. Serve with baby spinach & arugula sliced on top.

Nutrients Values: Fat 5.9g - Protein 11g - Carbs 24g - Fiber 5g - Calories 171

8.19 Roasted Beets and Asparagus Salad with Black Cherry Vinaigrette

PREP TIME: 25 Minutes

COOK TIME: 10 minutes

SERVES: 4 servings

DIFFICULTY LEVEL: Easy

INGREDIENTS:

- ½ cup vinegar with a fruity taste
- 1 quart of water
- 2 tablespoons arrowroot powder, dissolved in ¼ cup cold water
- 4 beets, medium red
- 20 asparagus stalks, cut into 1-inch diagonal pieces
- 4 cups soft-textured greens, cleaned
- 1 cup herbed "goat cheese."
- ½ cup walnuts, chopped
- 2 tbsp. fresh dill, chopped
- To taste freshly ground black pepper

DIRECTIONS

1. In a small saucepan, bring the vinegar and a cup of water to a boil.
2. When the water is boiling, mix in the arrowroot/cold water combination and cook for 2 minutes, stirring periodically.
3. Remove the vinaigrette from the stove and set it aside to cool at room temperature.
4. Remove the tops & tails of the beetroot, carefully wash them, and arrange them in a baking dish.
5. Cover the baking dish with ½ inch of boiling water, wrap with foil, & roast for an hour

at 400°F.

6. Remove the pan from the oven and set it aside to cool at room temperature.

7. Remove the skins from the beets by soaking them in cold water and rubbing them off.

8. Cut into ¼ -inch thick circular slices and combine in a mixing dish with ¼ cup vinaigrette.

9. Place 1 cup of greens, one-quarter of the asparagus pieces, & then the beetroot pieces on four separate dishes to make the salad.

10. Place a spoonful of the herbed "cheese" on each beetroot slice if preferred.

11. Drizzle with as much black cherry vinaigrette as you like.

12. Add the walnuts, dill, and freshly crushed black pepper to taste.

Nutrients Values: Fat 14g - Protein 11g - Carbs 20g –Fiber 6g - Calories 236

8.20 Quinoa Mango Salad

PREP TIME: 25 Minutes

COOK TIME: 15 minutes

SERVES: 4 servings

DIFFICULTY LEVEL: Easy

INGREDIENTS:

- 1 cup quinoa, dry
- 1 chopped cucumber
- 1 peeled and diced ripe mango or 2 pitted and sliced fresh peaches
- ¼ cup fresh basil leaves, coarsely chopped
- 2 quarts cherry or grape tomatoes, halved
- 2 tbsp. balsamic vinaigrette
- 1 ½ cup cooked garbanzo beans
- 5 oz. baby greens (mixed)

DIRECTIONS

1. Put quinoa in a fine-mesh strainer and rinse for a few seconds under cold water.

2. Bring 2 cups of water to a boil in a saucepan.

3. Reduce heat and add the quinoa.

4. Cover and cook for 15 minutes or until all of the liquid has been absorbed.

5. Mix cooked quinoa, basil, chickpeas, mango, cucumber, tomatoes, and vinegar in a large mixing bowl.

6. On top of mixed greens, serve.

Nutrients Values: Fat 3.3g - Protein 15g - Carbs 65g -Fiber 10.6g - Calories 335

8.21 Three Bean Mango Salad

PREP TIME: 25 Minutes

COOK TIME: 15 minutes

SERVES: 6 servings

DIFFICULTY LEVEL: Easy

INGREDIENTS:

- 1 ½ cup cooked cannellini beans drained and washed
- 1 (15-ounce) can of no-salt-added, or low-sodium kidney beans drained
- 1 (15-ounce) can of cooked chickpeas (garbanzo beans)
- ½ cup finely cut flat-leaf parsley
- 2 mangoes, peeled, pitted, & diced
- ½ red onion, finely chopped
- ½ red bell pepper, chopped
- ½ cup of water
- 1/3 cup apple cider vinegar
- Raw almonds (¼ cup) or raw almond butter (1/8 cup)
- A quarter cup of raisins
- 2 tablespoons mustard (whole grain)
- ½ teaspoon oregano, dry
- Mixed greens, 10 oz.

DIRECTIONS

1. Combine the bell pepper, beans, onion, parsley, and mangoes in a large mixing dish.
2. In a high-powered processor, combine the vinegar, water, oregano, almonds, mustard, & raisins until smooth.
3. Toss the beans in the dressing to coat them.
4. Allow the beans to soak up the taste of the dressing by chilling them for several hours.
5. On top of mixed greens, serve.

Nutrients Values: Fat 5g - Protein 15g- Carbs 55g - Fiber 12.5g - Calories 307

8.22 Detox Thai Tofu Salad

PREP TIME: 30 Minutes

COOK TIME: 10 minutes

SERVES: 4 servings

DIFFICULTY LEVEL: Easy

INGREDIENTS:

Salad

- Baby spinach leaves, 16 ounces
- 6 ounces trimmed snap peas
- 1 cup shredded carrots

- 1 cup purple cabbage, shredded
- 3 nicely chopped green onion stalks
- ½ cup chopped peanuts or cashews
- 1 big red or orange bell pepper, sliced
- 1 large ripe avocado, diced
- 1/3 cup

Sauce

- ½ cup creamy peanut butter
- 3 tablespoons soy sauce or Tamar
- 3 teaspoons rice vinegar
- 4 tablespoons lime juice
- 4 tablespoons maple syrup
- Three garlic cloves
- 1 ½ tablespoons ginger, minced
- 2 teaspoons red pepper flakes
- ½ cup of water
- 1 ½ teaspoon sesame oil
- 2 teaspoons soy sauce or tamari
- ½ tbsp cornstarch or tapioca flour
- 1 ½ tbsp cornstarch or tapioca flour

DIRECTIONS

1. Set the oven to 450 degrees Fahrenheit. Using parchment paper, line a baking sheet.
2. Tofu should be sliced into 1-inch thick squares. Arrange the tofu on a clean cloth in a single layer.
3. Cover the tofu with another towel and place something heavy (preferably a cast-iron skillet) on top for ten min to press it.

Peanut Sauce

4. Mix the vinegar, soy sauce, red pepper flakes, peanut butter, garlic, lime juice, syrup, water, ginger, and sesame oil in a blender.
5. Blend on high for 1 minute, or until smooth and creamy. If desired, add additional red pepper flakes to make it hotter.
6. Tofu should be diced into 1-inch (2.5 cm) chunks.
7. Drizzle one tablespoon of soy sauce over the tofu in a shallow dish.
8. Gently toss it with your hands, then drizzle with the leftover tablespoon of soy sauce.
9. Toss the tofu with the starch until it is evenly covered. Mix the tofu with ¼ cup of peanut dressing and toss gently to coat.

10. Place the tofu on the baking tray in a single layer, leaving space between each piece.

11. Bake for 5 mins, then flip and bake for further 5 minutes, or until golden brown and crisp.

12. Place the carrot, snap peas, spinach, onion, cilantro, cabbage, avocado, and bell pepper in a decorative pattern.

13. Toss with tofu and nuts before serving. The peanut dressing should be served on the side.

14. Just before serving, toss with the salad.

Nutrients Values: Fat: 14g – Protein 11g – Carbs 25g – Calories 260

CHAPTER 9: SMOOTHIES AND BEVERAGES RECIPES FOR INTERMITTENT FASTING

Below mention are very delicious recipes for healthy smoothies.

9.1 Berry Banana Smoothie

PREP TIME: 10 Minutes

COOK TIME: No

SERVES: 1 serving

DIFFICULTY LEVEL: Easy

INGREDIENTS:

- A single banana
- ½ cup soy, almond, or cannabis milk, unsweetened
- 1 cup strawberries, frozen
- 1 tablespoon chia seeds, ground
- 1 cup spinach or romaine lettuce

DIRECTIONS

1. In a high-powered mixer, combine all ingredients and mix till thick and creamy.
2. Enjoy.

Nutrients Values: Fat 7.6 g - Protein 10 g – Carbs 55 g – Fiber 14.6 g – Calories 302

9.2 Apple Smoothie with Oatberries

PREP TIME: 10 Minutes

COOK TIME: No

SERVES: 2 servings

DIFFICULTY LEVEL: Easy

INGREDIENTS:

- ½ cup soy, cannabis, or almond milk, unsweetened
- 1 cored apple
- 1 cup strawberries, organic
- 2 tablespoons rolled oats (old-fashioned)
- A pinch of cinnamon
- 1 tablespoon chia seeds, ground
- Pine nuts (1 tablespoon)
- 1 cucumber, tiny

DIRECTIONS

1. In a mixer, combine all ingredients.
2. Enjoy.

Nutrients Values: Fat: 8.5 g– Protein: 11 g – Carbs: 35 g –Fiber: 9.5 g - Calories: 23

9.3 Amazing Blended Smoothie

PREP TIME: 10 Minutes

COOK TIME: No

SERVES: 1 serving

DIFFICULTY LEVEL: Easy

INGREDIENTS:

- Baby greens, 8 oz.
- 1 peeled and seeded orange
- ¼ lemon juice

DIRECTIONS

1. In a high-powered mixer, blend the ingredients till thick and creamy.
2. Enjoy.

Nutrients Values: Fat0.8 g- Protein 4g - Carbs 24g - Fiber 7 g - Calories 106

9.4 Choco Cherries Smoothie

PREP TIME: 10 Minutes

COOK TIME: No

SERVES: 2 servings

DIFFICULTY LEVEL: Easy

INGREDIENTS:

- baby spinach, 4 oz.
- ½ cup soy, cannabis, or almond milk, unsweetened
- ½ cup juice from pomegranate
- 1 tablespoon cocoa powder
- 1 cup cherries, frozen
- A single banana
- 1 cup blueberries, frozen
- ½ teaspoon extract de Vanille
- 2 tbsp. flax seeds (ground)

DIRECTIONS

1. Grind the spinach with soy milk and juice in a normal blender.
2. Blend in the other ingredients for about 2 minutes, or until completely smooth.
3. Blend everything at once if you're using a high-powered blender.

Nutrients Values: Fat 5.5g – Protein 8g – Carbs 53g - Fiber 9.9g - Calories 270

9.5 Green Goblin

PREP TIME: 10 Minutes

COOK TIME: No

SERVES: 2 servings

DIFFICULTY LEVEL: Easy

INGREDIENTS:

- A dozen avocados
- A single banana
- Romaine lettuce, 5 oz.
- Baby spinach, 5 oz.

DIRECTIONS

1. Blend the avocado and banana in a blender or high-powered mixer, then put in the lettuce & spinach.
2. Blend till the mixture is thick and creamy.

Nutrients Values: Fat 8.3 g - Protein 5g – Carbs 24 g - Fiber 8.8 g - Calories 172

9.6 Boston Emerald Smoothie

PREP TIME: 10 Minutes

COOK TIME: No

SERVES: 2 servings

DIFFICULTY LEVEL: Easy

INGREDIENTS:

- Boston lettuce, 2 oz.
- 2 cups pineapple cubes (fresh or frozen)
- Three kiwis
- A dozen avocados
- A single banana

DIRECTIONS

1. In a high-powered mixer, combine all ingredients till thick and creamy.
2. Enjoy.

Nutrients Values: Fat 8.8g – Protein 6g- Carbs 57g– Fiber 12.3g – Calories 297

9.7 Orange Sherbet Blended smoothie

PREP TIME: 10 Minutes

COOK TIME: No

SERVES: 2 servings

DIFFICULTY LEVEL: Easy

INGREDIENTS:

- ½ cup soy, cannabis, or almond milk, unsweetened
- 1 big peeled orange
- Romaine lettuce, 6 oz.
- spinach, 6 ounces
- vanilla extract (two tablespoons)
- 10 cashews, whole and unprocessed
- 4–5 cubes of ice

DIRECTIONS

1. In a high-powered mixer, combine all ingredients and mix until thick and creamy.
2. Enjoy.

Nutrients Values: Fat: 8.9g - Protein: 9g Carbs: 22g - Fiber: 6.5g - Calories: 202

9.8 Purple Monster Smoothie

PREP TIME: 25 Minutes

COOK TIME: No

SERVES: 2 servings

DIFFICULTY LEVEL: Easy

INGREDIENTS:

- A single banana
- 2 cups pineapple chunks (fresh or frozen)
- 2 cups blueberries, frozen
- 2 Boston lettuce heads
- 1 tablespoon chia seeds, ground
- ½ cup of water

DIRECTIONS

1. In a high-powered mixer, combine all ingredients till smooth.
2. Adjust the amount of water to get the desired consistency.

Nutrients Values: Fat: 2.9g - Protein: 4g - Carbs: 55g - Fiber: 9.6g - Calories: 233

9.9 Apple Smoothie In Tea

PREP TIME: 5 Minutes (For steeping, 30 minutes required)

COOK TIME: 5

SERVES: 2 servings

DIFFICULTY LEVEL: Easy

INGREDIENTS:

- 1 cup rice milk, unsweetened
- 1 tea bag (chai)
- 1 peeled, cored, and chopped apple
- 2 quarts ice

DIRECTIONS

1. Heat the rice milk in a medium saucepan over medium heat for around 5 minutes or steaming.
2. Take the milk off the heat and steep the teabag in it.
3. Allow 30 minutes for the milk to cool in the fridge with the teabag, then remove the teabag and squeeze lightly to release all of the flavors.
4. In a blender, combine the milk, apple, and ice and mix till smooth.
5. Pour the mixture into two glasses and serve.

Nutrients Values: Fat 1g – Carbs 19g – Protein 1g - Calories 88

9.10 Smoothie With blueberry & Pineapple

PREP TIME: 15 Minutes

COOK TIME: No

SERVES: 2 servings

DIFFICULTY LEVEL: Easy

INGREDIENTS:

- 1 cup blueberries, frozen
- ½ cup of pineapple chunks
- ½ cup cucumber (English)
- ½ apple
- ½ cup of water

DIRECTIONS

1. In a blender, combine the water, cucumber, pineapple, apple, and blueberries and mix till creamy & smooth.
2. Pour the mixture into two glasses and serve.

Nutrients Values: Fat 1g – Carbs 22g - Protein 1g - calories 87

9.11 Smoothie Of watermelon & Raspberries

PREP TIME: 10 Minutes

COOK TIME: No

SERVES: 2 servings

DIFFICULTY LEVEL: Easy

INGREDIENTS:

- ½ cup red cabbage, cooked, chilled, and shredded
- 1 cup watermelon, diced
- ½ cup raspberries, fresh
- 1 pound of ice

DIRECTIONS

1. In a blender, pulse the cabbage for 2 minutes, or till it is nicely chopped.
2. Pulse for about 1 minute, or till the watermelon & raspberries are fully mixed.
3. Blend in the ice till the smoothie is thick and smooth.
4. Pour the mixture into two glasses and serve.

Nutrients Values Fat 0g – Carbs 11g – Protein 1g - : Calories 47

9.12 Juice from Cruciferous Plants (High Cruciferous Juice)

PREP TIME: 10 Minutes

COOK TIME: No

SERVES: 2 servings

DIFFICULTY LEVEL: Easy

INGREDIENTS:

- 3 carrots, medium
- 3 florets of cauliflower
- 1 apple, peeled and quartered
- kale leaves, 6–8
- A third of a cup of watercress with stems
- 2 cups broccoli stemmed

DIRECTIONS

1. Using a juicer, blend all of the ingredients.
2. Enjoy.

Nutrients Values: Fat 0.4g- Protein 3.5g - Carbs 14g – Fiber 3.9 - Calories 64

9.13 Antioxidant Power Juice

PREP TIME: 10 Minutes

COOK TIME: No

SERVES: 2 servings

DIFFICULTY LEVEL: Easy

INGREDIENTS:

- 4 leaves of kale
- 5 peeled carrots
- 2 bok choy stalks
- 1 apple, peeled and quartered
- 1 medium peeled beet
- A lemon squeeze

DIRECTIONS

1. Blend all of the ingredients in a juicer.
2. Enjoy.

Nutrients Values: Fat 0.4g – Protein 3g - Carbs 16 g – Fiber 4.1g - Calories 68

9.14 Detoxifying Green Tea

PREP TIME: 15 Minutes

COOK TIME: No

SERVES: 4 servings

DIFFICULTY LEVEL: Easy

INGREDIENTS:

- 1 kale bunch
- 2 cups lettuce leaves (romaine)
- 1 slice of cucumber
- 4 bok choy leaves
- 2 cups green tea, unsweetened
- 2 cups raspberries, frozen
- 2 cups frozen strawberries or cherries

DIRECTIONS

1. Juice the bok choy, kale cucumber, and romaine lettuce in a juicer to make green juice.
2. Combine the green tea and 2 cups of green juice in a mixing bowl.
3. Blend in a blender with frozen cherries, frozen strawberries, and frozen raspberries until smooth.

Nutrients Values: Fat 0.5g - Proteins 2g - Carbs 11g – Fiber 3.8g - Calories 48

9.15 Pomegranate Refresher

PREP TIME: 10 Minutes

COOK TIME: No

SERVES: 2 servings

DIFFICULTY LEVEL: Easy

INGREDIENTS:

- 1 pomegranate juice cup
- 1 cup organic strawberries, frozen or fresh
- 1 tablespoon lime juice or four kumquats
- 1 quart of water

DIRECTIONS

1. In a high-powered blender, combine all of the ingredients.
2. Enjoy.

Nutrients Values: Fat 0.1g – Protein 0.3g – Carbs 27g –Fiber 1.6g - Calories 113

9.16 Delicious Green Smoothie

PREP TIME: 15 Minutes

COOK TIME: No

SERVES: 1 serving

DIFFICULTY LEVEL: Easy

INGREDIENTS:

- 1 kiwi fruit, diced
- 2 ½ cucumbers, chopped

- 2 celery stalks, sliced
- 2 tbsp extra-virgin olive oil

DIRECTIONS

1. In a blender, combine all of the ingredients, along with some spice and 150ml water.
2. Pour the mixture into two glasses and serve right away.

Nutrients Values: Fat 0.5g - Proteins 6g - Carbs 15g – Fiber 6.8g - Calories 165

9.17 Smoothie with Spiced Mango

PREP TIME: 10 Minutes

COOK TIME: No

SERVES: 2 servings

DIFFICULTY LEVEL: Easy

INGREDIENTS:

- 1 mango, peeled, stoned, and cut into pieces
- 1 tbsp Greek yogurt (full-fat)
- ½ orange zest and juice
- ½ cup almond milk
- ¼ tsp. the ground cinnamon, with enough to serve
- ½ inch peeled and shredded root ginger
- A big pinch of turmeric powder

DIRECTIONS

1. In a blender, combine all of the ingredients.
2. Pour it into two glasses and garnish with a sprinkling of powdered cinnamon.

Nutrients Values: Fat 5.5g – Protein 8g – Carbs 53g - Fiber 9.9g - Calories 190

9.18 Smoothie with Coconut and Greens

PREP TIME: 10 Minutes

COOK TIME: No

SERVES: 2 servings

DIFFICULTY LEVEL: Easy

INGREDIENTS:

- 1 cup Coconut Molokai
- 1 cup frozen peaches, thawed
- 1 pound of spinach
- 2 tbsp. flaxseed meal

DIRECTIONS

1. Thaw the peaches until they are mushy but still frozen.
2. Blend for 2-3 minutes, or till very smooth, the, frozen peaches, Molokai Coconut, flax meal, and spinach. Taste and adapt to your personal preferences.
3. Immediately serve or refrigerate.

Nutrients Values: Fat: 0.4g - Carbs: 70g -Fiber: 9.2g – Protein 5.4g- Calories: 307

9.19 Turmeric Orange Juice

PREP TIME: 10 Minutes

COOK TIME: No

SERVES: 2 servings

DIFFICULTY LEVEL: Easy

INGREDIENTS:

- 4 peeled oranges
- 4 Carrots, big
- Removed a 2-inch section of Turmeric skin

DIRECTIONS

1. Everything should be washed and chopped to put into your blender.
2. Enjoy the juice!

Nutrients Values: Fat 0g – Protein 1g – Carbs 13g – Fiber 0g – Calories 55

9.20 Turmeric Refresher

PREP TIME: 10 Minutes

COOK TIME: No

SERVES: 2 servings

DIFFICULTY LEVEL: Easy

INGREDIENTS:

- ½ cup orange juice from Florida
- ½ inch piece of ginger, grated
- honey, 2 tbsp.
- 1 large pinch of turmeric powder

DIRECTIONS

1. Combine all of the ingredients in a mixing bowl and whisk until smooth.
2. Immediately pour into a small serving glass and consume.

Nutrients Values: Fat 0.7g – Protein 2.2g - Carbs 60.5g – Fiber 0.5g – Calories 241

CHAPTER 10: SOUPS & STEWS RECIPES FOR INTERMITTENT FASTING

Some recipes for delicious soups and stews are mentioned below.

10.1 Homemade Veggie Soup

PREP TIME: 20 Minutes

COOK TIME: 1 hour

SERVES: 4 servings

DIFFICULTY LEVEL: Easy

INGREDIENTS:

- 1 cup thinly chopped scallions
- 2 medium onions, chopped
- 2 cups mushrooms, chopped
- 2 medium tomatoes, chopped
- 3 garlic cloves, peeled and halved crosswise
- 4 carrots, diced
- 2 celery stalks, chopped
- Three bay leaves
- 1 cup fresh dill, chopped
- ½ Cup Fresh Parsley, Crumbled
- 6 black peppercorns, whole
- 1 teaspoon oregano, dry
- 14 quarts liquid

DIRECTIONS

1. Bring all of the ingredients to a boil in a big saucepan. Reduce the heat to low and cook for approximately 1 hour.
2. Remove any foam from the surface and discard it.
3. Remove the bay leaves and strain the broth, but keep the veggies to eat separately or purée to thickening soups or sauces.
4. Instead of using store-bought vegetable broth in soup recipes, try making your own.
5. It Can be stored in tiny containers for up to six months in the freezer.

Nutrients Values: Fiber 2.8g – Protein 3g - Carbs 9g - Fat 0.3g - Calories 43

10.2 Acorn Squash Stew with Brussels Sprouts

PREP TIME: 15 Minutes

COOK TIME: 15 minutes

SERVES: 4 servings

DIFFICULTY LEVEL: Easy

INGREDIENTS:

- 1 small sliced onion
- 6 garlic cloves, minced
- 1 small trimmed, cored, and finely sliced fennel bulb
- 2 cups peeled & cut into 34-inch pieces of acorn squash
- 8 ounces trimmed and halved brussels sprouts
- 4 cups vegetable broth (low sodium or no salt added)

- 2 teaspoons crushed fresh sage
- 1 tablespoon crushed fresh rosemary or 1 teaspoon crushed dried rosemary
- 1 cored and roughly chopped apple
- 6 apricots, dry and unsulfured, coarsely chopped
- ½ cup red kidney beans, cooked
- sherry vinegar, 1 tbsp
- to taste freshly ground pepper
- ½ cup dried veggies

DIRECTIONS

1. In a large saucepan, heat 1/8 cup water, add the onion and garlic, and water-sauté until soft, about 4 minutes.
2. Broth, rosemary, fennel brussels sprouts, squash, and sage are added to the pot.
3. Bring to a boil, then turn off the heat.
4. Cover and cook for 10 minutes or until the veggies are almost tender.
5. Combine the apple and apricots in a bowl. Cook for another 5 minutes, covered, or until the brussels sprouts are soft.
6. Heat through the beans and vinegar.
7. Season with salt and pepper.

Nutrients Values: Fat 2.3 g – Protein 15g – Carbs 48g – Fiber 11.8 g - Calories 246

10.3 Black forest Soup with Mushrooms in Cream

PREP TIME: 10 Minutes

COOK TIME: No

SERVES: 5 servings

DIFFICULTY LEVEL: Easy

INGREDIENTS:

- 2 pound fresh mushrooms, assorted, cut ¼ inch thick
- 2 garlic cloves, minced or crushed
- 2 teaspoons Provence herbs
- 5 pounds carrot juice (5 pounds carrots, juiced)
- 3 cups cannabis, soy, or almond milk, unsweetened, split
- 2 coarsely chopped carrots
- ¾ cup fresh or frozen corn kernels
- 2 medium onions, chopped
- 1 cup celery, chopped
- 3 leeks, quartered into 12-inch thick rounds
- No-salt seasoning mix that may be tweaked to taste Vegetable Zest

- ¼ cup cashews, uncooked
- 1 tablespoon lemon juice, freshly squeezed
- 1 tablespoon fresh thyme, chopped
- 2 teaspoons fresh rosemary, chopped
- 3 cups white beans, cooked
- ¼ cup finely chopped parsley, for garnish
- 5 ounces of baby spinach
- 1 cup dry beans

DIRECTIONS

1. Bring the carrot juice, 2 ½ cups milk, celery, onion, corn, carrots, leeks, and VegiZest or another no-salt seasoning mix to a boil in a large soup pot.
2. Combine the mushrooms, garlic, and herbes de Provence in a large mixing bowl.
3. Reduce the heat to low and cook for 30 minutes, or until the veggies are soft.
4. Puree the cashews and the remaining 12 cups of milk in a food mixer or high-powered blender.
5. Half of the soup broth and veggies and the lemon juice, thyme, and rosemary should be added now.
6. Blend until the mixture is smooth and creamy.
7. Return the soup stock to the pot once it has been pureed.
8. Add the beans, spinach, and mushrooms that have been sautéed.
9. Heat the spinach until it has wilted.
10. Serve with parsley as a garnish.

Nutrients Values: Fat 5.1g - Protein 18g – Carbs 53g –Fiber 11g - Calories 305

10.4 Broccoli Mushroom Bisque

PREP TIME: 10 Minutes

COOK TIME: 30 Minutes

SERVES: 4 servings

DIFFICULTY LEVEL: Easy

INGREDIENTS:

- 1 broccoli head, sliced into florets
- 8 ounces sliced mushrooms
- 3 coarsely chopped carrots
- 1 cup celery, roughly chopped
- 4 garlic cloves, minced
- 1 onion, diced
- a couple of tablespoons of Mrs. Dash spice combination (no salt)

- 2 quarts of carrot juice (2 pounds of carrots, juiced)
- 4 cups of water
- Nutmeg (1/2 teaspoon)
- ½ cup cashews, raw
- ½ cup pine nuts
- ½ cup pine nuts

DIRECTIONS

1. In a soup saucepan, combine all of the ingredients apart from the cashews and pine nuts.
2. Cook for 20 minutes, or until the veggies are just cooked, and covered.
3. Blend two-thirds of the soup broth and veggies with the cashews and pine nuts in a food mixer or high-powered blender until smooth and creamy.
4. Before serving, return to the saucepan and reheat.

Nutrients Values: Calories 339 – Protein 13g – Carbs 37g – Fat 19g – Fiber 7.8g

10.5 Cheesy Kale Soup

PREP TIME: 15 Minutes

COOK TIME:15 Minutes

SERVES: 4 servings

DIFFICULTY LEVEL: Easy

INGREDIENTS:

- ½ cup split yellow peas
- 1 cup sliced mushrooms
- 1 onion, diced
- 2 quarts of carrot juice (2 pounds of carrots, juiced)
- 15 ounces tomato sauce (no salt added or reduced-sodium)
- 1 ½ pound kale greens, stiff stems, and central ribs removed chopped coarsely
- ½ cup cashew butter (raw)
- A teaspoon of nutritious yeast

DIRECTIONS

1. Cover yellow split peas with about 2 ½ cups of water in a pressure cooker and cook on high pressure for 8 to 12 minutes.
2. Cook for 1 minute on high pressure with the other ingredients apart from cashew butter & nutritional yeast.
3. After the pressure has been released, puree the soup with cashew butter.
4. Before serving, sprinkle with nutritional yeast.

Nutrients Values: Protein 18g – Carbs 58g – Fat 99g – Fiber 13g - Calories 363

10.6 Crunchy Sweet Potato Stew

PREP TIME: 10 Minutes

COOK TIME: 20 Minutes

SERVES: 2 servings

DIFFICULTY LEVEL: Easy

INGREDIENTS:

- 1 thickly sliced onion
- ½ cup stewed tomatoes with liquid
- 2 big garlic cloves, chopped
- 1 big peeled sweet potato, sliced into ½ -inch chunks
- 1 cup (prepared or canned) garbanzo beans with no salt added or minimal sodium
- ¾ teaspoon rosemary (dried)
- ½ inch thick circles from 1 medium zucchini
- 1 Tablespoon Mrs. Dash, seasoning with no salt
- 1/3 cup dry beans

DIRECTIONS

1. Two tablespoons of water, heated in a saucepan.
2. Put the onion & water and cook for 5 minutes, or until the onion is slightly softened, dividing the slices into rings.
3. Cook for 1 minute after adding the garlic.
4. To prevent scorching, add water as needed.
5. Add the rosemary, garbanzo beans, & sweet potato to the stewed tomatoes with juice.
6. Stir occasionally while the mixture comes to a simmer.
7. Cook for 5 minutes with the lid on. Toss in the zucchini.
8. Cook, occasionally turning, till sweet potatoes are cooked, about 15 minutes.
9. Mrs. Dash is used to season the dish.

Nutrients Values: Fat 3.6g – Protein 9g – Carbs 50g – Fiber 7.9g - Calories 253

10.7 Medley of Corn and Beans

PREP TIME: 15 Minutes

COOK TIME: 25 Minutes

SERVES: 5 servings

DIFFICULTY LEVEL: Easy

INGREDIENTS:

- 2 cups corn (fresh or frozen)
- ½ cup great northern or cannellini beans, cooked

- 1 ½ cup kidney beans, cooked
- 1 chopped red bell pepper
- 1 medium carrot, peeled and sliced
- 1 big sliced onion
- 2 garlic cloves, chopped
- 1 medium peeled and sliced potato
- 3 quarts liquid
- No-salt seasoning mix that may be tweaked to taste
- 2 tbsp. dulse powder
- 1 teaspoon Mrs. Dash spice (no salt added) or to taste
- 1 teaspoon Provence herbs
- Baby spinach, 14 oz.
- ½ cup dry beans of each kind

DIRECTIONS

1. In a soup saucepan, combine all ingredients except the spinach. Bring the water to a boil.
2. Reduce to a low heat setting, cover, and cook for 20 minutes, or until soft veggies.
3. Cook for another 5 minutes, or till the spinach has wilted.

Nutrients Values: Fat: 1.8g - Protein: 19g – Carbs: 63g - Fiber: 15.1g - Calories: 316

10.8 Asparagus Cream Soup

PREP TIME: 10 Minutes

COOK TIME: 10 Minutes

SERVES: 4 servings

DIFFICULTY LEVEL: Easy

INGREDIENTS:

- 2 teaspoons No-salt seasoning blend, adjusted to taste
- 1 pound fresh asparagus, chopped
- VegiZest by Dr. Fuhrman
- 2 c. liquid
- 1 tbsp Bragg Liquid Amino Acids
- 1 cup soy, almond, or cannabis milk, unsweetened
- ¼ cup cashews, uncooked
- ¼ cup almonds (raw)
- 4 dates with pits

- Garnish with chopped fresh cilantro

DIRECTIONS

1. In a soup pot, cook Bragg Liquid Aminos, VegiZest or no-salt seasoning blend, water, asparagus and until tender.

2. In a high-powered blender, combine almonds, liquid, soy milk, asparagus, cashews, and dates, & until smooth. Before serving, garnish with cilantro.

Nutrients Values: Fat 9.3g – Protein 9g- Carbs 30g – Fiber 5.2g – Calories 223

10.9 Creamy Zucchini Soup

PREP TIME: 10 Minutes

COOK TIME: 30 Minutes

SERVES: 4 servings

DIFFICULTY LEVEL: Easy

INGREDIENTS:

- 1 big onion, diced
- 3 garlic cloves, chopped
- 2 pounds zucchini, cut (about 5 medium)
- 1 teaspoon dried basil
- ½ tsp. dried thyme
- ½ teaspoon oregano, dry
- 4 cups low-sodium or no-salt vegetable broth
- 1/4 cup cashews (raw) or 18 cups cashew butter (raw)
- 2 cups kernels of corn
- 4 cups spinach (baby)
- 1/4 teaspoon freshly ground black pepper, or to taste

DIRECTIONS

1. In a large soup saucepan, combine the thyme, garlic, oregano, basil, onion, and, as well as vegetable broth.

2. Bring to a boil, lower to low heat, and continue to cook for another 25 minutes until the zucchini is soft.

3. Put into a food blender or high-powered mixer, add the cashews, and mix thick and creamy.

4. Return the soup to the pot, add the corn & baby spinach, and cook until the spinach is wilted.

5. If necessary, add more water to get the desired consistency. a pinch of black pepper

Nutrients Values: Fat 5.4g – Protein 10g – Carbs 33g – Fiber 6.9 – Calories 195

10.10 Fuhrman's Famous Soup

PREP TIME: 10 Minutes

COOK TIME: 30 Minutes

SERVES: 10 servings

DIFFICULTY LEVEL: Easy

INGREDIENTS:

- 1 cup split peas and beans, dry
- 4 cups of water
- 6–10 zucchini, medium
- 5-pound juiced carrots
- 2 celery bunches, juiced
- 1 teaspoon Mrs. Dash
- 2 tablespoons Dr. Fuhrman's VegiZest seasoning with no salt
- 3 leek stalks, finely chopped
- 4 medium onions, chopped
- Stiff stems and central ribs removed from 2 bunches of kale, collard greens, or other greens
- 1 cup cashews, raw
- 2 ½ cups fresh mushrooms, chopped

DIRECTIONS

1. In a very big saucepan over low heat, combine the split peas, beans, and water.
2. Bring to a boil, then lower to low heat and continue to cook.
3. Place the zucchini in the saucepan pot. Toss in the carrot, celery, Vegi Zest, and Mrs. Dash.
4. Blend the kale, leeks, & onions with a little of the soup liquid in a blender.
5. Fill the soup pot with this mixture.
6. Take off the wilted zucchini with tongs and puree them with the cashews in a blender until smooth.
7. Return the mixture to the soup pan. Continue to boil the beans until they are soft, approximately Two hours total cooking time.

Nutrients Values: Fat 7.4g – Protein 16g – Carbs 56g – Fiber 12g – Calories 322

10.11 Quick Homemade Tomato Gazpacho

PREP TIME: 10 Minutes

COOK TIME: No

SERVES: 4 servings

DIFFICULTY LEVEL: Easy

INGREDIENTS:

- 1 medium cucumber
- 3 Roma tomatoes
- 1 red bell pepper, chopped
- ½ onion, red
- 1 serrano pepper (or jalapeno) for a milder flavor
- ½ cup basil leaves
- ½ cup parsley (fresh)
- 2 cups tomato sauce (canned)
- 1 cup of water
- ¼ cup extra virgin olive oil, split
- 1 tablespoon white wine vinegar
- 2 tbsp balsamic vinaigrette
- 1 lemon's juice (about two tablespoons)
- 2 cloves garlic

DIRECTIONS

1. The tomatoes should be quartered, the cucumber should be peeled and sliced, the pepper should be de-seeded and quartered, and the onion cut in half.

2. 1 tomato, two cucumber slices, and 1/4 teaspoon pepper are set aside.

3. In a blender, combine the vegetables that you haven't placed aside.

4. Blend the remaining ingredients on high till smooth and creamy, utilizing just three tablespoons of oil.

5. Chill in the refrigerator. Add the remaining ingredients to a bowl and finely chop them.

6. Add a sprinkle of salt, a few more herbs (if you have them), and the remaining one tablespoon of oil.

7. To mix, stir everything together. Pour the soup into dishes when ready to serve.

8. Enjoy! Garnish with the "diced" salad and a pinch of fresh pepper.

Nutrients Values: Fat 14g– Protein 3g – Carbs 15g – Fiber 4g – Calories 196

10.12 Detoxifying Beet & Gazpacho Soup

PREP TIME: 15 Minutes

COOK TIME:45 Minutes

SERVES: 10 servings

DIFFICULTY LEVEL: EASY

INGREDIENTS:

- 3 beet bulbs, medium size (ends cut)

- ¼ cup freshly squeezed lime juice (plus 1 teaspoon fresh lemon zest for garnish)
- 1 quart of water
- a quarter-cup of pine nuts
- 2 garlic cloves
- 2 full peeled oranges (cut into segments and garnish with one teaspoon of orange zest)
- Sea salt that hasn't been refined (to taste)
- cucumber and radishes, finely diced (for garnish)

DIRECTIONS

1. Preheat the oven to 350 degrees Fahrenheit.
2. Each beet bulb should be wrapped in parchment paper.
3. On a thick cookie sheet, put the wrapped beet bulbs.
4. Beets should be roasted for 25 to 30 minutes or until they are just soft.
5. Remove the beets from the oven, carefully unwrap them, and set them aside to cool.
6. Coarsely slice the beets once they've cooled enough to handle.
7. Twelve diced beets, lemon juice, and water in a high-powered blender Blend until completely smooth.
8. Return to the processor and add the remaining beets. Process the garlic, orange, and pine nuts segments until completely smooth.
9. To taste, season with salt. Place the soup in a large mixing basin, cover it, and refrigerate for 2 to 3 hours.
10. Serve with cucumber and radish slices as garnish.

Nutrients Values: Fat 0.7g– Protein 6.2g – Carbs 3g – Fiber 9g – Calories 153

CHAPTER 11: APPETIZERS & SNACKS RECIPES FOR INTERMITTENT FASTING

Below mention are the recipes for snacks & appetizers.

11.1 Baked Garlic Dip

PREP TIME: 15 Minutes

COOK TIME: 1 hour

SERVES: 6 servings

DIFFICULTY LEVEL: EASY

INGREDIENTS:

- 1 peeled and sliced into eighths big sweet onion
- 8 cloves of garlic
- 2 teaspoons extra virgin olive oil
- ½ cup sour cream (mild)
- 1 tablespoon lemon juice, freshly squeezed
- 1 tablespoon fresh parsley, chopped
- 1 teaspoon fresh thyme, diced
- Black pepper, freshly ground

DIRECTIONS

1. Set the oven to 425 degrees Fahrenheit.
2. Mix the garlic and onions with the olive oil in a small bowl.
3. Place the garlic and onions on a piece of aluminum foil and loosely wrap them in a bundle.
4. Place the foil wrap on a medium baking tray and bake it for 15 minutes.
5. Bake, for approximately 50 minutes to an hour, or till the veggies are aromatic and golden.
6. Allow 15 minutes for the packet to cool after removing it from the oven.
7. Combine the sour cream, lime juice, thyme, parsley, & black pepper in a medium mixing bowl.
8. Carefully open the foil wrapper and place the veggies on a chopping board.
9. Chop the veggies and toss them in with the sour cream. To mix, stir everything together.
10. Before serving, cover the dip and chill it in the fridge for 1 hour.

Nutrients Values: Fats 3g - Carbs 5g – Protein 1g - Calories 44

11.2 Baked Eggplants

PREP TIME: 20 Minutes

COOK TIME:30 Minutes

SERVES: 6 servings

DIFFICULTY LEVEL: EASY

INGREDIENTS:

- 1 medium eggplant, half and scored on the cut sides with a crosshatch pattern
- 1 tablespoon extra virgin olive oil, with a little extra for brushing
- 1 big peeled and sliced sweet onion
- 2 halved garlic cloves
- 1 teaspoon cumin powder
- 1 teaspoon coriander powder

- A quarter-cup of lemon juice
- Black pepper, freshly ground

DIRECTIONS

1. Set the oven to 400 degrees Fahrenheit. Line two baking pans with parchment paper.
2. Brush one baking sheet with olive oil & arrange the eggplant pieces cut-side down.
3. Combine the garlic, onion, 1 tbsp olive oil, coriander, and cumin in a small bowl.
4. On the other baking sheet, spread the seasoned onions.
5. Bake the onions for approximately twenty minutes as well as the eggplant for thirty min, or till softened and browned on both baking pans.
6. Scoop the aubergine flesh into a dish after removing the veggies from the oven.
7. Toss the garlic and onions with the eggplant on a chopping board and coarsely chop.
8. Add the lime juice and pepper to taste. Warm or chilled is fine.

Nutrients Values: Fat 2g – Carbs 6g – Protein 1g - Calories 45

11.3 Dip With Cheese & Herbs

PREP TIME: 20 Minutes

COOK TIME: NO

SERVES: 8 servings

DIFFICULTY LEVEL: EASY

INGREDIENTS:

- 1 pound of cream cheese
- ½ cup rice milk, unsweetened
- ½ scallion, coarsely cut green part alone
- 1 tablespoon fresh parsley, chopped
- 1 tablespoon basil leaves, chopped
- 1 tablespoon lemon juice, freshly squeezed
- 1 teaspoon garlic, minced
- ½ teaspoon fresh thyme, chopped
- ¼ teaspoon black pepper, freshly ground

DIRECTIONS

1. Combine the cream cheese, milk, fresh basil, scallions, parsley, lime juice, thyme, garlic, and pepper in a medium mixing bowl.
2. Refrigerate the dip for up to one week in an airtight container.

Nutrients Values: Fat 10g – Carbs 3g – Protein 2g – Calories 108

11.4 Kale Chips

PREP TIME: 20 Minutes

COOK TIME:25 Minutes

SERVES: 6 servings

DIFFICULTY LEVEL: EASY

INGREDIENTS:

- kale, 2 cups
- 2 teaspoons extra virgin olive oil
- ¼ tsp. chili powder
- A pinch of cayenne

DIRECTIONS

1. Set the oven to 300 degrees Fahrenheit. Set aside 2 baking sheets lined with parchment paper.
2. Remove the kale stems before tearing the leaves into 2-inch bits. Wash and dry the kale well.
3. Pour olive oil over the kale in a large mixing dish.
4. Rub the kale with the oil with your hands, making sure each leaf is well coated.
5. Toss the kale with cayenne pepper and chili powder to completely mix.
6. On each baking sheet, place the prepared kale in a single layer. Make sure the leaves aren't overlapping.
7. Bake the kale for 25 to 30 minutes, turning the pans once, or till crisp & dry.
8. Remove the pans from the oven and let the chips cool for five min on the tray.
9. Serve right away.

Nutrients Values: Fat: 2g - Carbs: 2 g - Protein: 1 g - Calories: 24

11.5 Tortilla Chips With Cinnamon

PREP TIME: 15 Minutes

COOK TIME:10 Minutes

SERVES: 6 servings

DIFFICULTY LEVEL: EASY

INGREDIENTS:

- 2 tbsp sugar (granulated)
- ½ teaspoon cinnamon powder
- 1 tsp. nutmeg, ground
- 3 flour tortillas (6 inches)

DIRECTIONS

1. Coat the tortillas with cooking spray. Set the oven to 350 degrees Fahrenheit.
2. Using parchment paper, line a baking sheet.
3. Combine the sugar, nutmeg, and cinnamon in a small bowl.

4. Spray both surfaces of the tortillas with cooking spray and place them in a clean workspace.

5. Using a pastry brush, evenly coat each side of the tortilla with cinnamon sugar.

6. Place the tortillas on the baking sheet, and cut them into 16 wedges each.

7. Roast the tortilla wedges for approximately 10 minutes, rotating once or until crisp.

8. Cool the chips completely before storing them in an airtight jar at ambient temperature for approximately a week.

Nutrients Values: Fat: 1g -Carbs: 9g - Protein: 1g - Calories: 51

11.6 Corn With Sweet & Spicy Kettle

PREP TIME: 5 Minutes

COOK TIME: 5 Minutes

SERVES: 8 servings

DIFFICULTY LEVEL: EASY

INGREDIENTS:

- 3 tablespoons extra virgin olive oil
- 1 cup kernels of popcorn
- ½ cup sugar (brown)
- A pinch of cayenne

DIRECTIONS

1. Add the olive oil and some popcorn seeds to a big saucepan with a cover over medium heat.

2. Lightly shake the saucepan till the popcorn seeds pop.

3. Toss in the remaining kernels as well as the sugar in the saucepan.

4. Shake the pot frequently while popping the kernels till they are all done.

5. Remove the popcorn from the saucepan and place it in a large mixing dish.

6. Serve the popcorn with a dash of cayenne pepper.

Nutrients Values: Fat: 6g - Carbs: 30g – Protein: 3g – Calories: 186

11.7 Ice Pops With Blueberries & Cream

PREP TIME: 10 Minutes

COOK TIME: NO

SERVES: 6 servings

DIFFICULTY LEVEL: EASY

INGREDIENTS:

- 3 cups blueberries (fresh)
- 1 teaspoon lemon juice, freshly squeezed
- ¼ cup rice milk, unsweetened

- ¼ cup sour cream (mild)
- ¼ cup sugar, granulated
- ½ teaspoon vanilla extract (pure)
- ¼ teaspoon cinnamon powder

DIRECTIONS

1. Puree the berries, lime juice, rice milk, sour cream, sugar, vanilla, and cinnamon in a blender until smooth.
2. Fill ice pop molds partially with the mixture and freeze for 4 hours, or until extremely solid.

Nutrients Values:; Fat: 1 g - Carbs: 18g - Protein: 1g - Calories : 78

11.8 Ice Milk With Candied Ginger

PREP TIME: 20 Minutes

COOK TIME: 15 Minutes

SERVES: 4 servings

DIFFICULTY LEVEL: EASY

INGREDIENTS:

- 4 cups rice milk, vanilla
- ½ cup sugar, granulated
- 1 (4-inch) piece peeled and thinly sliced fresh ginger
- ¼ teaspoon nutmeg powder
- ¼ cup candied ginger, coarsely chopped

DIRECTIONS

1. Combine the sugar, milk, & fresh ginger in a medium saucepan over moderate flame.
2. Heat the milk mixture for approximately 5 minutes, or till it is almost boiling, stirring gently.
3. Reduce to low heat and cook for fifteen minutes.
4. Remove the milk from the stove and stir in the nutmeg powder. To infuse the taste, let the mixture settle for 1 hour.
5. To remove the ginger, filter the milk mixture through a fine strainer into a medium dish.
6. Let the mixture in the fridge cool fully before adding the candied ginger.
7. In an ice cream machine, freeze the ginger ice according to the manufacturer's instructions.
8. Freeze the final dessert in a sealed jar for up to three months.

Nutrients Values: Fat: 1g - Carbs: 24g - Protein: 0g - Calories: 108

11.9 Cookies With Meringue

PREP TIME: 15 Minutes

COOK TIME:35 Minutes

SERVES: 4 servings

DIFFICULTY LEVEL: EASY

INGREDIENTS:

- 4 egg whites
- 1 cup sugar (granulated)
- 1 teaspoon vanilla extract (pure)
- 1 teaspoon extract (almond)

DIRECTIONS

1. Set the oven to 300 degrees Fahrenheit. Set aside two baking sheets lined with parchment paper.
2. Whisk the egg whites till stiff peaks form in a medium stainless steel mixing dish.
3. One tablespoon of granulated sugar at a time, whipping thoroughly after each addition to integrating, until all of the sugar is utilized & the meringue is stiff and smooth.
4. Combine the vanilla and almond extracts in a mixing bowl. Put the meringue mixture onto the baking pans with a tablespoon, spreading the cookies equally.
5. Bake for approximately 30 minutes or until the cookies are crisp. Take the cookies out of the oven and place them on wire racks to cool.
6. Keep the cookies at ambient temperature for up to a week in an airtight container.

Nutrients Values: Fat: 0g - Carbs: 8g - Protein: 1g - Calories: 36

11.10 Bread Made with Corn

PREP TIME: 10 Minutes

COOK TIME:20 Minutes

SERVES: 10 servings

DIFFICULTY LEVEL: EASY

INGREDIENTS:

- ¼ cup all-purpose flour
- 1 ¼ cup yellow cornmeal
- 1 tablespoon baking soda
- ½ cup sugar, granulated
- Two eggs
- 1 cup rice milk, unsweetened and unfortified
- 2 tablespoons extra virgin olive oil

DIRECTIONS

1. Set the oven to 425 degrees Fahrenheit. Set aside an 8-by-8-inch baking tray that has

been lightly sprayed with cooking spray.

2. Combine the flour, cornmeal, baking soda replacement, and sugar in a medium mixing dish.

3. Beat up the vegetables, rice milk, & olive oil in a small dish until well combined.

4. Combine the wet and dry ingredients in a mixing bowl and whisk until thoroughly mixed.

5. Fill the baking dish partly with batter and bake for 20 minutes, or till browned and cooked through.

6. Warm the dish before serving.

Nutrients Values: Calories 198 – Fat 5g – Carbs 34g – Protein 4g

11.11 Chicken Crostini With Roasted Red Pepper

PREP TIME: 10 Minutes

COOK TIME:5 Minutes

SERVES: 4 servings

DIFFICULTY LEVEL: EASY

INGREDIENTS:

- 2 tablespoons extra virgin olive oil
- ½ teaspoon garlic, minced
- 4 French bread slices
- ½ cup chopped fresh basil
- 1 roasted red bell pepper, chopped
- 4 ounces cooked chicken fillet, shredded

DIRECTIONS

1. Set the oven at 400 degrees Fahrenheit. Aluminum foil should be used to line a baking pan.

2. Combine the olive oil & garlic in a small bowl. Brush the olive oil mixture on both sides of each slice of bread.

3. Set the toast on the baking pan and bake for about 5 minutes, rotating once, or till golden and crisp on both sides.

4. Combine the red pepper, chicken, & basil in a medium mixing dish.

5. Serve the red pepper mix on top of each toasted bread piece.

Nutrients Values: Fat 8g – Carbs 19g – Protein 9g - Calories 184

CHAPTER 12: DESSERTS RECIPES FOR INTERMITTENT FASTING

Here are few dessert recipes.

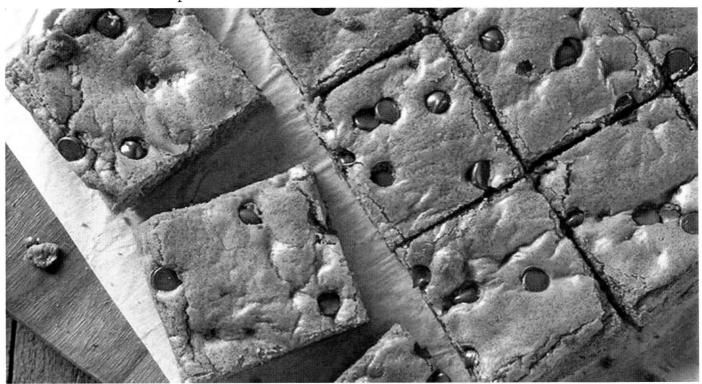

12.1 Granita D'Apple Tart

PREP TIME: 15 Minutes

COOK TIME: 15 Minutes

SERVES: 4 servings

DIFFICULTY LEVEL: EASY

INGREDIENTS:

- ½ cup sugar, granulated
- ½ cup of water
- 2 cups apple juice, unsweetened
- ½ cup lemon juice, freshly squeezed

DIRECTIONS

1. Dissolve the sugar in water in a medium saucepan over medium flame.

2. Raise the mixture to a boil, then reduce to low heat and continue to cook for 15 minutes, or till the liquid has been reduced by half.

3. Take the pan off the heat and transfer the mixture into a big shallow metal pan.

4. Allow 30 minutes for the liquid to cool before adding the lemon juice and apple juice.

5. Preheat the oven to 350°F. Put the skillet in the freezer. After 1 hour, use a fork to smash up any ice cubes that have developed in the liquid. Scrape the sides of the container as well.

6. Return the pan to the freezer for another 20 minutes, stirring and scraping to create slush.

7. After around 3 hours, when the mixture is frozen and appears like crushed ice, serve.

Nutrients Values: - Fat 0g – Carbs 0g - Protein 0g- Calories 157

12.2 Sherbet With Lime & Cream

PREP TIME: 5 Minutes

COOK TIME:15 Minutes

SERVES: 8 servings

DIFFICULTY LEVEL: EASY

INGREDIENTS:

- 2 c. liquid
- 1 cup sugar (granulated)
- 3 tbsp lemon zest (distributed)
- ½ cup lemon juice, freshly squeezed
- 1 lime, zest
- 1 lime's juice
- ½ cup heavy cream (whipped)

DIRECTIONS

1. Put the water, sugar, and two tablespoons lime zest in a large saucepan over medium flame.

2. Raise the mixture to a boil, lower to low heat and continue to cook for 15 minutes.

3. Add the remaining one tablespoon lime zest, lime juice, l to the mixture in a large mixing bowl.

4. Refrigerate the mixture for 3 hours or until it is cool.

5. Pour the batter into an ice cream machine after whisking in the heavy cream. Follow the manufacturer's directions for freezing.

Nutrients Values: Fat 6g – Carbs 26g – Protein 0g - Calories 151

12.3 Snow Cone With Vanilla Tropical

PREP TIME: 15 Minutes

COOK TIME:5 Minutes

SERVES: 4 servings

DIFFICULTY LEVEL: EASY

INGREDIENTS:

- 1 cup peaches in a can
- 1 pineapple cup
- 1 cup strawberries, frozen
- water (six tablespoons)
- 2 tbsp. sugar (granulated)
- 1 tbsp extract de Vanille

DIRECTIONS

1. Bring the strawberries, peaches, pineapple, water, and sugar to a boil in a large saucepan over medium flame.
2. Lower the heat and cook the mixture for 15 minutes, stirring often.
3. Remove the pan from the stove and set it aside for 1 hour to cool properly.
4. Add the vanilla extract and puree the fruit in a blender or food processor.
5. Purée the mixture until smooth, then pour it into a 9-by-13-inch glass baking tray.
6. Put the dish in the freezer overnight, covered. When the fruit combination has completely frozen, scrape the sorbet with a fork until flaky flavored ice forms.
7. Fill four serving bowls halfway with ice flakes.

Nutrients Values: Fat: 0g – Carbs : 22g - Protein: 1g – Calories: 92

12.4 Pavlova With Peaches

PREP TIME: 30 Minutes

COOK TIME: 1 hour

SERVES: 8 servings

DIFFICULTY LEVEL: EASY

INGREDIENTS:

- 4 big room-temperature egg whites
- A quarter-teaspoon of cream of tartar
- 1 cup sugar (superfine)
- ½ teaspoon vanilla extract (pure)
- ½ cup canned peaches in juice, drained

DIRECTIONS

1. Set the oven at 225 degrees Fahrenheit. Set aside a baking sheet lined with parchment paper.

2. In a large mixing bowl, whisk the egg whites until soft peaks form, about 1 minute.

3. Add the tartar cream and mix well. One tablespoon at a time, add the sugar till the egg whites are firm and glossy.

4. Don't beat up too much. Blend in the vanilla extract.

5. Spoon the meringue evenly onto the baking tray to make eight circles.

6. Make a hole in the center of each round with the bottom of the spoon.

7. Bake for 1 hour till a medium brown crust forms on the meringues.

8. Please turn off the oven and let the meringues cool overnight in it.

9. Place the meringues on serving dishes after removing them off the sheet.

10. Serve the peaches in the middle of the meringues, equally distributed.

11. Any leftover meringues can be kept for up to a week in a sealed container.

Nutrients Values: Fat 0g – Carbs 32g – Protein 2g - Calories 132

12.5 Peaches Baked With Cream Cheese

PREP TIME: 10 Minutes

COOK TIME: 15 Minutes

SERVES: 4 servings

DIFFICULTY LEVEL: EASY

INGREDIENTS:

- 1 cup plain cream cheese
- ½ cup Meringue Cookies, crushed (here)
- ¼ teaspoon cinnamon powder
- 1 tsp. nutmeg, ground
- 8 peach halves in juice from the can
- Honey (two tablespoons)

DIRECTIONS

1. Set the oven to 350 degrees Fahrenheit. Set aside a baking sheet lined with parchment paper.

2. Combine the cream cheese, meringue cookies, nutmeg, and cinnamon in a small mixing bowl.

3. Fill the holes in the peach halves equally with the cream cheese mixture.

4. Bake for approximately 15 minutes, or until the peaches are tender and the cheese has melted, on the baking sheet.

5. Place two peaches on plates from the baking sheet and sprinkle with nectar or honey before serving.

Nutrients Values: Fat 20g – Carbs 19g – Protein 4g - calories 260

12.6 Custard With Sweet Cinnamon

PREP TIME: 20 Minutes

COOK TIME: 1 hour

SERVES: 6 servings

DIFFICULTY LEVEL: EASY

INGREDIENTS:

- Grease the ramekins with unsalted butter.
- ½ cup rice milk, unsweetened
- 4 quail eggs
- ¼ cup sugar, granulated
- 1 teaspoon vanilla extract (pure)
- ½ teaspoon cinnamon powder
- Cinnamon sticks to serve as a garnish

DIRECTIONS

1. Set the oven to 325 degrees Fahrenheit. Set aside 6 (4-ounce) ramekins that have been lightly greased and placed in a baking dish.
2. Whisk the sugar, eggs, rice milk, cinnamon, and vanilla in a large mixing bowl until smooth. Into a pitcher, strain the batter through a fine sieve.
3. Distribute the custard mixture evenly among the ramekins. Fill the baking dish halfway up the edges of the ramekins with b
4. oiling water, being careful not to allow any water into the ramekins.
5. Bake for 1 hour, or till the custards are done, and a knife poked in the center comes out clean.
6. Remove the ramekins from the water and take out the custards from the oven.
7. Cool for 1 hour on wire racks before transferring to the fridge to chill for a further hour.
8. If desired, serve every custard with a cinnamon stick.

Nutrients Values: Fat: 4g - Carbs: 14g - Protein: 4g - Calories: 110

12.7 Raspberry Brulee

PREP TIME: 10 Minutes

COOK TIME:5 Minutes

SERVES: 4 servings

DIFFICULTY LEVEL: EASY

INGREDIENTS:

- ½ cup sour cream (mild)
- ½ cup plain cream cheese
- ¼ cup brown sugar, split
- ¼ teaspoon cinnamon powder

- 1 cup raspberries, fresh

DIRECTIONS

1. The oven should be preheated to broil.
2. Combine the cream cheese, sour cream, cinnamon, and two tablespoons of brown sugar in a small mixing bowl and beat for about 4 minutes, or until the mixture is extremely smooth and fluffy.
3. Divide the raspberries evenly between 4 (4-ounce) ramekins. Smooth the tops of the berries with the cream cheese mixture.
4. Cover the ramekins and keep them in the refrigerator until you're ready to enjoy the dish.
5. ½ tbsp brown sugar, equally distributed over each ramekin. Set the ramekins on a baking tray and broil till the sugar is caramelized and golden brown, about 4 inches from the heat source.
6. Remove the baking sheet from the oven. Allow 1 minute for the brûlées to cool before serving.

Nutrients Values: Fat 13g – Carbs 16g – Protein 3g - Calories 188

12.8 Couscous Pudding With Vanilla

PREP TIME: 20 Minutes

COOK TIME:20 Minutes

SERVES: 6 servings

DIFFICULTY LEVEL: EASY

INGREDIENTS:

- ½ cup rice milk, unsweetened
- ½ cup of water
- ½ cup honey 1 vanilla bean, split
- ¼ teaspoon cinnamon powder
- 1 couscous cup

DIRECTIONS

1. In a large saucepan over medium heat, whisk the rice milk, water, and vanilla bean.
2. To infuse the vanilla flavor into the milk, bring the milk to a moderate simmer, decrease the heat to low, and leave the milk to cook for 10 minutes.
3. Turn off the heat in the pot. Remove the vanilla bean and scoop the seeds from the shell into the heated milk with the point of a sharp knife.
4. Put the cinnamon and honey in a mixing bowl. Mix in the couscous and set aside for 10 minutes, covered.
5. Fluff the couscous with a fork before serving.

Nutrients Values: Calories Fat 1g – Carbs 77g – Protein 6g

12.9 Pudding With Honey Bread

PREP TIME: 15 Minutes

COOK TIME: 40 Minutes

SERVES: 6 servings

DIFFICULTY LEVEL: EASY

INGREDIENTS:

- ½ cup rice milk, unsweetened
- Two eggs
- 2 egg whites, big
- ¼ cup of honey
- 1 teaspoon vanilla extract (pure)
- 6 cups white bread, cubed

DIRECTIONS

1. Set aside an 8-by-8-inch baking sheet that has been lightly greased with butter.
2. Mix together the rice milk, whites, eggs, vanilla, and honey in a medium mixing dish.
3. Stir in the bread cubes until they are evenly covered. Cover the mixture with plastic wrap and place it in the baking dish.
4. Refrigerate the dish for a minimum of 3 hours before serving. Set the oven to 325 degrees Fahrenheit.
5. Bake the pudding for 30 to 35 minutes, until light brown and a knife poked in the center come out clean.
6. Warm the dish before serving.

Nutrients Values: Fat 3g – Carbs 30g – Protein 6g - Calories 167

12.10 Ruhab Crumble

PREP TIME: 15 Minutes

COOK TIME: 30 Minutes

SERVES: 6 servings

DIFFICULTY LEVEL: EASY

INGREDIENTS:

- 1 cup flour (all-purpose)
- ½ cup sugar (brown)
- ½ teaspoon cinnamon powder

- ½ cup room temperature unsalted butter
- 1 cup rhubarb, chopped
- 2 peeled, cored, and thinly sliced apples
- 2 tbsp. sugar (granulated)
- A couple of teaspoons of water

DIRECTIONS

1. Preheat the oven to 325 degrees Fahrenheit. Set aside an 8-by-8-inch baking dish that has been lightly

greased with butter.

2. Combine the flour, sugar, and cinnamon in a small mixing dish and whisk well. Rub in the butter with your fingertips until the mixture resembles coarse crumbs.
3. Cook the rhubarb, apple, sugar, and water in a medium saucepan over medium heat for about 20 minutes or until the rhubarb is tender.
4. Fill the baking dish halfway with the fruit mixture and equally distribute the crumble on top.
5. Preheat the oven to 350°F and bake the mixture for 15 to 20 minutes, or until lightly browned.
6. Serve immediately.

Nutrients Values: Fat 23g – carbs 60g – Protein 4g - Calories: 450

12.11 Chia Pudding With Mango, Turmeric, And Coconut

PREP TIME: 15 Minutes

COOK TIME: 30 Minutes

SERVES: 6 servings

DIFFICULTY LEVEL: EASY

INGREDIENTS

- 1 cup frozen mango or one big mango, diced
- 1 quart of coconut milk
- Chia seeds, five teaspoons
- 1 tbsp maple syrup (or honey)
- A quarter teaspoon of turmeric
- Topping: coconut yogurt
- Topping of coconut chips
- Topping: kiwifruit

DIRECTIONS

1. In a blender, puree the mango until smooth. If you're going to use frozen mango, thaw it first.
2. In a mixing bowl, combine the mango mixture and the remaining ingredients and whisk until no lumps remain.
3. Allow for 5 minutes before stirring again. Refrigerate overnight, covered.
4. Serve in two glasses with a dollop of natural or coconut yogurt, mango and kiwi chunks, and a sprinkling of coconut.

Nutrients Values: Fat 9g – carbs 29g – Protein 5g - Calories: 208

12.12 Greek Yogurt with Walnuts and Fruit

PREP TIME: 15 Minutes

COOK TIME: 30 Minutes

SERVES: 6 servings

DIFFICULTY LEVEL: EASY

INGREDIENTS

- 3 apricots (dry), coarsely chopped
- A third of a cup of plain nonfat Greek yogurt
- ½ teaspoons walnuts, chopped

DIRECTIONS

1. In a dish, combine the yogurt and the honey.
2. Add the apricots and walnuts and mix well.
3. Enjoy.

Nutrients Values: Fat 2.7g – carbs 9.8g – Protein 8.5g - Calories: 93

CONCLUSION

Rather than a traditional diet, the intermittent fasting diet plan is a way of eating. An intermittent fasting diet emphasizes when you eat, rather than what you eat as per conventional diet plans. You alternate through cycles of extreme or full-calorie restriction, in other terms, periods of fasting and healthier eating while following this eating style. The duration of these calorie-restricted and healthy-eating cycles differs according to one's personal desire.

Intermittent fasting (IF) is one of the most famous health and fitness phenomena in the world right now. People are using it to lose weight, boost their health, and ease their lives. Intermittent fasting is also a very easy and effective lifestyle approach. During a fast, several people report feeling healthier and gaining more energy. Furthermore, intermittent fasting also lowers the risk of developing certain chronic diseases. Intermittent fasting helps you consume and enjoy a broad range of foods because it does not restrict which foods to eat and which to skip, instead it focuses on a well-balanced, nutrient-dense diet. Many studies have shown that it may have a significant impact on the body and brain and that it can also help you live longer. According to the International Food Information Council (IFIC), about 10% of more than 1,000 Americans aged 18 to 80 who were surveyed in early April practice intermittent fasting, making it one of the most popular lifestyles. The way we eat food to sustain our fitness, performance, and recovery becomes more important as we get older. Good eating is easy, but it may be hard to manage and maintain. A woman's health declines tremendously during her pre-menopausal and post-menopausal phases. Their living standard suffers as a result of this. As intermittent fasting is a code to longevity, the intermittent fasting diet plan is structured in such a way that your body can remain balanced while fasting and even increase your life span. So, with a few supportive workouts and certain dietary options, check out this fantastic lifestyle approach, as intermittent fasting is an excellent way to reduce serious health conditions that women often face in their late 40s. As a result, this book is a must if you want to improve your fitness and longevity. You are not going to be disappointed.

Made in United States
North Haven, CT
30 May 2023

37177576R00113